"Tighten your seat belt. You are in for s as you fly through Rick Stephens' life This internationally known entrepreneu and failures, guiding you to find the s to your own 'Promised Land.' You will learn faith-based business and life lessons from your armchair, lessons Rick paid for in the 'School of Hard Knocks.'"

Merrill J. Oster
Founder, Pinnacle Forum
Author, *You Can Change the World*

"Not often does one get to celebrate a life well-lived while the man is still on this side of eternity, but that's exactly what I did while reading each page of this book about my good friend and Pinnacle Forum brother, Rick Stephens. This excellently written and engaging book is packed with real-life drama and profound wisdom born from life's challenges and trials. Rick manages to capture his reader's mind with valuable business insights—while also gripping the heart—as he humbly and transparently shares his life's tragedies, trials, and triumphs. It's almost like a cross between Ken Blanchard's *One Minute Manager* and the movie *It's a Wonderful Life*. With every turn of the page, one sees the golden thread of God's favor and blessings falling upon this man who sought to put God first and to make every aspect of his life—his business, family, and friends—an act of worship to Him. Well done!"

Stephen Cervera
President, Mission Fuel, Inc.
Former Systems Engineering Manager, Apple, Inc.

"*In Plane Sight* is a powerful and inspiring true story about a man, Rick Stephens, who has been used by God to bless hundreds of employees, friends, and family. Rick's remarkable life story is told with Scripture and examples that describe his journey from humble beginnings to building the world's leading hobby company. By listening to God, obeying and believing, he overcame obstacles, made mistakes, and persisted . . . honoring his deep faith every step of the way. It is an inspiring entrepreneurial story, filled with guidance for any leader."

Cordia Harrington
CEO, The Bakery Cos.

"Rick Stephens' new book, *In Plane Sight*, inspired, educated, informed, and entertained me. Talk about bang for the buck! I have the highest regard for Rick as a person, Christian, and business entrepreneur. What a gift for all of us that he has taken the time to share his experiences and beliefs about these three identities! *In Plane Sight* is a great life story, business journey, and testament to faith in God and the wonders it brings. For me, a special feature of the book is that it is 'confessional' in the best sense of that word: honest, authentic, and completely candid. Rick has achieved a lot. But he is a humble person, so the tone is never about him. It is about his wife, Jeanene, and their family, his colleagues and co-workers in the company he founded, and the benefactors of his and Jeanene's generosity. Above all, *In Plane Sight* is about Rick's relationship with God, how it developed, and why it has mattered. When I received *In Plane Sight*, I dove in immediately and read it from cover to cover in a couple of days. It is that engaging. Thank you, Rick!"

B. Joseph White
President Emeritus, University of Illinois
Dean Emeritus, Ross School of Business, University of Michigan

"*In Plane Sight* is an inspirational, courageous reflection and I highly recommend it. Rick's clear writing and no-excuse style provides an easy, clear read that leaves no doubt about his faith and God's role in his interesting and successful career."

James Leonard, MD
CEO CarleHealth

"In *In Plane Sight*, Rick Stephens offers a compelling and transparent retrospective of a successful entrepreneur and Kingdom-minded leader with a heart for God and people. Through tests and triumphs, he reveals the essence of his principles-based philosophy to work and life: do the right thing, do the thing right, and involve God every step of the way. In doing so, he inspires and equips us to lead in a manner that brings out the best in people. Thank you, Rick, for your gift of wisdom and example."

Dennis J. Trittin
President of LifeSmart Publishing, LLC and author of
What I Wish I Knew at 18: Life Lessons for the Road Ahead

"Rick believes that in business you need a significant change every five to eight years, but one thing does not change—our walk with God. In this book, Rick shares how he has walked with God through every trail, tragedy, loss, mistake, and victory. Rick has been a blessing in my life for forty years, and I have witnessed many of the stories in this wonderful book. I will share this book with many who do not know Rick personally, but will benefit from his message of faithfulness."

Rev. Dr. Edgell Franklin Pyles, PhD
Chaplain Emeritus, Snowmass Chapel

"Rick Stephens' book, *In Plane Sight*, is one of the most beautiful books I have read in many years. Rick talks eloquently about how God has been by his side in every aspect of his life: the successes and the challenges, the beautiful treasured moments and the tragic ones. He makes it clear that God has guided all the important decisions he has made.

The amazing story of Rick's life is that, although he has depended on God, he has not let that replace his hard work to start and lead a successful business or his love and devotion to his family and friends. His religious grounding permeates every minute of his life from the moment he met two strangers while in college until today. This kind of unswerving faith is moving, and makes this book an important read no matter what your religious background is."

Phyllis M. Wise, CEO, Colorado Longitudinal Study
Former Chancellor, University of Illinois, Urbana-Champaign
Former Provost and Interim President, University of Washington

"When my good friend Rick asked me for my critical review of *In Plane Sight*, I called to urge him to publish it to a wider business audience. By telling his story so candidly, Rick provides many valuable 'lessons learned' for young business leaders: be absolutely clear about your mission, empower all members of your team, ask for help when you need it, and, after careful analysis of strategic options, be willing to take major risks. And, at the heart of it all, is Rick's real-life relationship with God, which adds dimension and depth to his career in business.

I highly recommend this book to all members of the Young Presidents Organization, which both Rick and I have been part of, and those in leadership positions in any business or nonprofit. I can't wait to give *In Plane Sight* to my two adult boys, who are both young entrepreneurs!"

James W. Light
Co-founder of Chaffin Light Associates

IN
PLANE
SIGHT

IN
PLANE
SIGHT

Making Faith the Bedrock
of Your Career

RICK STEPHENS

NEW YORK

LONDON • NASHVILLE • MELBOURNE • VANCOUVER

IN PLANE SIGHT

Making Faith the Bedrock of Your Career

Published in New York, New York, by Morgan James Publishing. Morgan James is a trademark of Morgan James, LLC. www.MorganJamesPublishing.com

Morgan James BOGO™

A **FREE** ebook edition is available for you or a friend with the purchase of this print book.

CLEARLY SIGN YOUR NAME ABOVE

Instructions to claim your free ebook edition:
1. Visit MorganJamesBOGO.com
2. Sign your name CLEARLY in the space above
3. Complete the form and submit a photo of this entire page
4. You or your friend can download the ebook to your preferred device

ISBN 9781631955372 paperback
ISBN 9781631955389 ebook
Library of Congress Control Number:
2021932493

Cover Design by:
Chris Treccani
www.3dogcreative.net

Editorial and Book Design by:
Inspira Literary Solutions

Morgan James PUBLISHING

with...

Habitat for Humanity® Peninsula and Greater Williamsburg

Morgan James is a proud partner of Habitat for Humanity Peninsula and Greater Williamsburg. Partners in building since 2006.

Get involved today! Visit
MorganJamesPublishing.com/giving-back

*To my eight grandchildren – Lars Kellner, Ellie Barker,
Paige Bokelman, Steffen Kellner, Kate Barker, Liza Bokelman,
Hans Kellner, and Claire Bokelman. You are growing up to be
kind, compassionate, talented, and well-rounded young men and
women. Thank you for allowing me to be part of your life.*

Table of Contents

Acknowledgments

Like most good things in my life, this book would never have come about without the love, support, and wisdom of my extraordinary partner in life, Jeanene. If you knew how private and humble she is, you would understand what a challenge it has been for her to see our life laid out in such detail for all to examine. Thank you Jeanene, for giving me permission to share some of our most intimate experiences of life with the hope that others might benefit. From reading early drafts that were way too wordy and messy, to helping me navigate the most difficult subjects, to cover design advice and everything in between, you are as responsible for the end product as I am. I never cease to be amazed at your grace, beauty, faith, empathy for others, and fun-loving spirit. Thank you for being my companion, friend, lover, and wife for these (almost) fifty years.

I also want to thank my daughters—Jill Kellner, Carrie Barker, and Marnie Bokelman—for planting the seed for this book when they gifted me a Grandfather's Journal for my birthday. What strong and faithful young women you have become. Without your thoughtfulness and creativity, *In Plane Sight* may never have come to pass. I will love you unconditionally forever.

In Plane Sight started as a rambling journal to my grandchildren, condensed slightly into more of a book, and presented to Arlyn Lawrence of Inspira Literary Solutions. Arlyn was so gentle and kind as she explained important little things, like a chapter should be closer to four thousand words than ten thousand! She and her accomplished associate, Heather Sipes, did an awesome job of eliminating all the boring detail and sharpening the story to make my ramblings actually readable and interesting. Thank you, Arlyn and Heather, for all the work you did behind the scenes to make me look good.

What excitement I felt when David Hancock of Morgan James Publishing showed interest in my book. Thank you, David, for giving this first-time author a chance by publishing *In Plane Sight* under your brand. I hope it will be a successful addition to your impressive library of titles.

I want to thank Tim Johnson, my long-time friend, mentor, and comrade in our journey of faith together. You really annoy me sometimes because you are so faithful to God and me that I often feel convicted for not being as strong for others as you are for me. But, of course, I appreciate your continual prayers, encouragement, advice, and inspiration that have been so important to me these past twenty-seven years. Thank you for cheering me on throughout the process of writing this book, and for being my friend.

A special thank you to Joe Thomas and Phil Reed, for your professional input regarding how this book might be used most effectively. Your ability to zero in on principles that readers might be able to apply to their own life and provide questions to facilitate discussion have been invaluable. Your encouragement and direction often came at just the right time to keep me on track.

Credit for the title of this book goes entirely to Karen Wandell. It was serendipitous, one relaxing evening at Jeff and Charlotte's home, when I first met their son Michael's fiancé (now wife). In time, the conversation turned to my book. As soon as I finished describing a short version of my story and the theme of the book, Karen said, "I have the title for you! It should be called *In Plane Sight!*" She was right. Since my career was linked to RC airplanes and the invisible Spirit of

God becoming real to me, it was a no-brainer. I will never forget how perceptive you were at a moment's notice. Thank you, Karen.

Finally, this story would not have been possible without the help of those closest to the heart of Horizon. I want to thank my brother, Larry, who was by my side from beginning to end and the one whom I can always trust. Eric Meyers, Janet Ottmers, Debra Love Clark, Roger Rhodes, and Terri Kirby were all absolutely crucial to our success. In fact, without their talent, commitment, and support, I'm convinced Horizon Hobby never would have made it. And to the many other Horizonites who grasped our vision and lived it out—thank you for making Horizon *special*.

Foreword

In the twenty years since co-founding Lead Like Jesus with my long-time friend, Ken Blanchard, it has been my privilege to meet hundreds of outstanding Christian leaders who are seeking to reflect the image of Christ in their lives and leadership.

Rick Stephens is one such leader. When Rick asked me to write a foreword for his autobiography, I was pleased to say yes.

A few years ago, I had the opportunity to spend several days with Rick and key members of the Horizon Hobby executive team. It was a special time to get to know Rick and meet some of the people who are important to his life story.

In Plane Sight is a wonderfully rich source of insights into what it means to have a living, active faith as the bedrock of a God-honoring life and career. Rick shares his life story as a testimony to the blessings he has received. He speaks from a heart of gratitude about God's influence on his personal and professional journey in building an industry-leading organization.

Rick, by his own admission, is a man of action. He loves life and is quick to praise God as the author and source of his joy. Faith, prayer, love, gratitude, and God's Word are the spiritual underpinnings of *In Plane Sight*.

It is also a practical guide to the value of hard work, compelling values and vision, well-grounded ethical practices, and a highly motivated desire to serve the common good. There is much to learn from

Rick's story about the power of trust, honoring your contracts, listening to truth tellers in your life, and trusting your own best instincts.

What I love about *In Plane Sight* is meeting the people that Rick honors for having influenced his journey. His truth tellers, mentors, encouragers, challengers, rescuers, and inspirers are an awesome group. In a class all by themselves are his wife, Jeanene, and his brother, Larry, who have supported Rick on his journey.

The enduring truth of Rick Stephens' story is the faith-tested testimony of what God can do with and through a willing heart. Putting God in the center of your life is the message Rick brings forward into plain sight from a life well-lived and well-led. This message will change your life. This book can be a new beginning. It was for me.

Phil Hodges
Co-founder of Lead Like Jesus
Co-author of *Lead Like Jesus*, *Lead Your Family Like Jesus*, and *Servant Leader*

Introduction

When I turned sixty, my three daughters gave me the best birthday gift I've ever received. They gave me a "Grandfather's Journal" and asked me to write down my life story so their children, present and future, will know who their grandfather really was. I took it as a huge compliment that the girls considered my story worth telling. And what a privilege for me to be able to share it with the next generation and maybe even beyond.

I took my assignment seriously and began writing, and writing, and writing. Ten years later, I had accumulated quite a tome of real-life experiences that, hopefully, would encourage and empower my grandchildren someday. What I had written also became the center-piece for speaking engagements during this time, and eventually led to this book.

I'm grateful to my daughters for many reasons, but the respect and honor bestowed upon me with this one gift is right at the top of the list. My "Grandfather's Journal" made me aware of just how much I love life! And what I love most about life is that *the story isn't my story as much as it's God's story*. It's a story about how He has been in and around me every step of the way, lovingly nudging me toward the best life possible instead of settling for less. He had a plan for me from before the day I was born (Jeremiah 29:11), and, as much as I've allowed Him the chance to work, He has fulfilled it. It's been exciting, adventurous, purposeful, and successful beyond my wildest dreams. I couldn't have written this script, but God could—and He did.

In spite of all the mistakes I've made, God has done amazing things in my life. He prepared me to start my own company from the basement of our home and, somehow, it became a multi-million-dollar business with over seven hundred people and locations around the globe. He provided for me a lovely wife who has been by my side for fifty years. Our daughters have grown up to be strong young women who chose superb husbands and with them brought into this world a total of eight unique, talented, gifted children whom we adore.

With a successful business/career, loving family, and faith in God, Jeanene and I have been blessed with everything this world has to offer. *Yet, this is only the tip of the iceberg when it comes to living life to its fullest.* The *abundant life* God has in store for us is not confined to the borders of the world. Abundant life emerges when we look at life differently—through the lens of the spirit God has made within us to live in communion with Him.

We are created with two complementary forms of existence—our physical life and our spiritual life. Our physical life is quite tangible and obvious. In it we experience successes, failures, happiness, sadness, joy, grief, pain, excitement, love, fear and all the rest. These emotions are REAL and cannot be ignored. Our spiritual life is not so tangible. It exists and is just as REAL as our physical life, but it can be ignored/left dormant. However, when activated, our spiritual life puts all the tangible activity and emotions we experience in the world into the perspective of our Creator. With it, we experience our physical life in terms of eternity and live in communion with God. That is the way life was intended to be for us.

Living life within the borders of the world leaves so much on the table—it's like experiencing only half of life, and it's not the best half. I want to live a full and complete life—a life in which my spiritual life is real, alive, and paramount to everything else, not like the one I used to live where faith is compartmentalized as one of several important priorities of my physical life. I want my faith to be part of an intimate spiritual life with God's point of view. The experiences I'm going to share with you have given me a taste, just a taste, of what it might be like to consistently live like this.

Albert Einstein said, "There are two ways to live your life. One is as though nothing is a miracle. The other is as though everything is a miracle." I see the amazing things that have happened to me as miracles designed and made real by God Himself. He has been the hero of my story from the beginning. Perhaps something in the way He has worked in and through me, an often disobedient and fallible man, will resonate with you, too, and inspire you to investigate this abundant life for yourself.

1

Foundations

I raced to the hospital in a frenzy, already thinking about how I would tend to Nelda's every need, nurse her back to health, and draw even closer to her than before. When I got to the emergency room, I asked at the nurse's station if I could see Nelda Alexander, but they wouldn't give me any information. All I knew was a car had been hit by a train and my girlfriend had been in that car. The nursing staff directed me to a waiting room, where I sat for almost two hours with no information.

Nelda was pretty, talented, smart, humble, fun, and a wonderful person to be around. We'd been dating for a year and always had a great time together. I was captivated by how kind she was to everyone, especially those less popular than herself. There was something special about Nelda. I knew she went to church on her own (I went only when forced), and believed in God, but I didn't understand what that meant. I figured it must have something to do with her kindness and fun-loving spirit. Nelda was my first love.

Finally, the family remembered I was there and came into the waiting room. I jumped up. "How is she? Is she okay? What can I do to help her? Will she get out of the hospital tonight?" The questions tumbled out of my mouth.

Nelda's mother quietly explained through tears that Marsha (the driver) had a broken leg. Debbie (Nelda's sister) was being treated for a fractured hand and was to be released, but Nelda's neck had been broken by the impact (the train had struck her side of the car), and she had died at the scene. Nelda was dead.

I felt like someone had just smacked me hard in the face. Stunned, I thought, *"No! This isn't the way it's supposed to be! For two hours I've been planning how I would be there by Nelda's side every moment as she recovered. She's only seventeen, for heaven's sake! It can't be true! Why did she have to die when the others are going to be all right?"* It was more than my seventeen-year-old mind could absorb. I didn't understand. And I had no idea how much Nelda's death would impact my life.

The family asked me to be a pallbearer at the funeral. This was all so foreign to me. I didn't know what to say. I felt so close to Nelda that being a pallbearer seemed to somehow undervalue my love for her. But, after talking to my parents, I decided the right thing was to honor the family's wishes. Nelda wore the same elegant green dress she had worn just two weeks earlier when I took her to the Homecoming Dance. I bought another white orchid for her as I'd done before. It was a sad and confusing time.

I was still in a daze the next spring when my friends were applying to colleges and making plans. I made no plans, didn't even consider applying to colleges. I'm not sure what I thought would happen after graduation, but I didn't really care. My parents just expected me to find work like they had done when they were my age—no one in my family had ever gone to college.

In fact, when my sister and brother-in-law, Joanne and Tom, suggested I attend college, it was the first time I'd ever really thought about it. It was already July, but Tom thought I still had a chance to get into Northern Illinois University (NIU). He helped me fill out the application and in early August I received a letter of acceptance.

Little did I know that God's hand was in this, and that NIU would be the place where the pieces of my shattered life would begin to come back together.

A Chance Encounter

In the 1960s, college freshmen had to live in a campus dormitory. However, because of my last-minute application, it was too late for me to get into a dorm, so Tom took me to Dekalb to look for a place to live. We found an off-campus apartment and two weeks later I moved in. Not surprisingly, the old house I found to live in had only upper classmen—mostly seniors who all knew each other. They didn't have much time for a freshman stranger. I was lost, alone, and still very confused.

Two weeks into the first semester I sat in the Student Union with my studies and a cup of coffee before me. (Even way back then, I worked best at a coffee shop, outside of home.) Two young men walked by my table. I saw them slow down and then circle back.

"Hey, how's it going?" asked one of the guys, looking more than a little bit awkward as he stood in front of me. "Do you mind if we sit down and talk with you?"

He was tall with short hair and glasses, conservatively dressed and not a person with whom I'd likely strike up a conversation. But, I was looking for a friend, any friend, so I instantly said yes. It was not your average conversation. Shortly after we all introduced ourselves, they asked me, quite directly, "If you were to die tonight, do you know for certain where you would go?"

It turned out they were men on a mission: they were with Campus Crusade for Christ (Cru) and wanted to make sure I was assured of my eternal destiny. Honestly, I was more concerned about what I was going to do Friday night, but I listened anyway.

Capitalizing on the uncertainty of my spiritual fate, combined with my apparent need for companionship, they opened up a booklet called *The Four Spiritual Laws* and proceeded to explain it to me. They told me that:

1. God loved me and wanted to have a relationship with me (John 3:16).

2. But, I was rejecting God and creating a chasm between us by ignoring/disregarding Him and devoting myself to doing what I wanted to do (Romans 3:23).

3. I deserved spiritual death for my rejection of God; however, His love is so great that He actually allowed His pure, innocent Son to die in my place, to pay the price for what I had done (and would do) wrong and bridge the gap (Romans 6:23).

4. God gave His Son up as a gift to me. I just had to decide whether I wanted to accept His gift of spiritual life through Christ . . . or not (Revelation 3:20).

Suddenly, it all "clicked." This was consistent with everything I'd ever heard or read about God. It was similar to what my mother had told me (she had taken my sister, brother, and me to church when we were kids, though Dad was never much interested). It explained what I had seen in Nelda's life that was so special. It lined up with what I understood the Bible promised, and what I was feeling inside. It all made perfect sense to me and I wanted to do something about it. But what? I believed it, but how could I ever experience it?

I thought I was already a pretty good guy—kind, nice, humble—but I could see now that wasn't what God was looking for. God wanted to have a *personal relationship* with me, one in which He would love me and I would love Him. It wasn't about keeping score of good and bad things done; it was about having regard for and trust in Him as my Creator, my Father, and my Friend.

The message was clear: God did all of that for me and now I had to decide: accept His gift of Jesus as the sacrifice that paid the price for my disobedience . . . or procrastinate, put it off, and say "No, I don't want Your gift, God." If I were to open the gift, I would enjoy a personal relationship with God and a life covered in joy and peace, because the gap between us had been bridged. If I rejected it, I would remain focused on myself and His gift of an abundant life would be left there, on the table, unopened.

I rolled this around in my head for a few weeks and finally decided I needed to give it a try. It was time for me to accept the gift God was handing to me. So I said, "I don't fully understand it, God, but in general this all makes perfect sense. I ask You to forgive me for going my own way without You and, through the sacrifice of your Son, I accept your gift of spiritual life. Help me now to understand it."

I was still the same person with the same personality, same desires, same strengths and weaknesses, and same selfishness to deal with. But, I knew something big was different. Somehow, for the first time, I felt that I not only had a physical life on Earth to live, but a spiritual life that ran parallel and it would live forever. I was on my way.

Getting Connected

The Cru guys suggested the best way to start getting connected would be to attend their weekly meetings and meet some people on this same journey with God. I did for a short while and learned that showing some love and respect for God really did work. It made me feel more purposeful. The more time I devoted to getting to know Him, the better I felt.

It was at a Cru meeting that I met Dave Larsen. Dave was a tall, thin, good-looking guy with a bit of a raspy voice that was actually pleasant and comforting. He was also involved with another Christian organization, the Navigators. Cru is known best for evangelism, telling people about Jesus and inviting them to begin a relationship with Him. The Navigators are known best for deep discipleship training. They encourage one-on-one discipleship where a more mature Christian befriends a new Christian and helps him/her grow in a relationship with Christ. This is what Dave Larsen did for me.

Dave became my friend. We started meeting together regularly to study the Bible and learn more about God. He taught me the Navigators' Hand illustration that breaks down five methods of getting to know God through His Word—hearing, reading, studying, memorizing, and praying/meditating. Dave showed me this is how we spend time with God, how we get to know God personally, and how we become able to actually live a life of meaning, peace, and joy.

Dave and I met regularly during my freshman year at NIU and roomed together my sophomore year. For two years, Dave was my best friend and mentor. He poured himself into helping me come into a closer personal relationship with God.

Near the end of my freshman year, Dave suggested I go to a Navigator summer training program. I needed to work to make enough money for the next year of school, but I really wanted more of God, too. So, I worked half the summer and the other half went to Maranatha Bible Camp in North Platte, Nebraska with other students from around the country. We worked during the day cleaning and maintaining the camp (free labor). Nights and weekends we had Bible studies, speakers, music, and fun events. Learning more about Christ was our focus for those six weeks and it was powerful.

At Maranatha I met other students just like me, not knowing a lot about God but wanting to know more. Most of my time was spent painting old buildings they used as cabins for kids' camps. One day, we were painting around some windows when we saw a shiny new white van pull in. Two weeks earlier, we had been told the old van Maranatha used to transport campers around the area had quit working for good. Camp leaders asked the staff and volunteers to pray that God would provide a van to replace the old one. So, we prayed and, sure enough, here comes a new van. Word was an anonymous donor had sent a check out of the blue for just enough money to buy this eleven-seat van, even though he or she didn't know of the specific need.

We were all excited and praised God for the van, but I had a lot of questions. I'd never seen anything like this. Was it just a coincidence? Is God like a vending machine that dispenses goodies when we "put in" prayer? What kind of person gives that kind of money anonymously? Was it all a trick, like a cult would perform to attract followers? How does God choose when to say yes to prayer and when to say no?

I discussed it at length with the other students, but never came to any conclusions. However, it was a powerful example that God used to form my thinking about Him and "giving" in the decades that followed.

As I learned more about God, I began to understand that *He is always working in my life.* Psalm 139 says God knew us before we were formed in our mother's womb. I was beginning to see how that can be. He is God, creator of all things, and He created me as His adopted son. I'm His child and He loves me at least as much as my own mother and father did. That kind of love is unconditional. He wants only the best for me where it really matters. He wants me to love Him back, but He doesn't force me to. It's my choice. Regardless, He touches my life every moment of every day to show His love and encourage me to live in a way that gives me the most joy, peace, and love I can possibly experience. That's all He wants. And everything He does in and around me is designed to help me get there.

So, being born to Modine and Eli was not an accident, nor was anything else in my life. God knew Modine would introduce me to Jesus. He knew Nelda's death would cause me to realize I shouldn't wait until I was old to consider Him. He knew how lonely I was and those two guys from Cru would stop at my table in the Union that day and talk to me about Him. He knew all about the circumstances that led me to Dave Larsen. He knew about Maranatha Bible Camp. And He knew that the new van experience would impact my thinking for a lifetime.

Change in Course

Returning to school for my sophomore year was an exciting time for me. Classes surrounding my finance major were actually fun—something I'd never experienced before in school. Turns out I loved business and at the same time felt like I was on a good path of getting to know God better. Dave and I shared an apartment and did everything together.

As the school year was ending, I decided to go to a Navigator leadership training camp for the summer at the University of Maryland. I needed to make money to pay for the next year of school, but this program was a mix of work and training. We stayed in dorms in College Park, just inside the Beltway of Washington, DC, and attended Navigator meetings/events at night and on weekends. But, we were expected to find full-time jobs and work during the day.

The only job I could find that started right away was at a landscaping firm and I took it. I cut grass all day long, every day. I took pride in cutting straight lines and admiring the nicely manicured lawn when completed. It paid reasonably well, but I needed to make more. After two weeks, some fellow students told me where I might find a better paying job, so I went after it. I became a general laborer for a construction firm building a high rise. It was hard work, but was a union job that was not at a fast pace. Now I could make enough to cover my next year of school, although taking pride in my work was not encouraged in this job.

One of my friends at the Navigators leadership camp attended the University of Illinois. We talked about the value of a degree from the U of I versus NIU. I had not thought of transferring until then, but the U of I was only twenty miles from home and many of my high school friends went to school there. It sounded appealing in a lot of ways. In July, I decided to send an application for a transfer from one state school to another. Just before I left College Park that summer, I was accepted at the University of Illinois.

My transfer was a big blow to Dave Larsen. We had planned on being roommates again my junior year and his "calling" seemed to be continuing to disciple me in my faith. Dave was very disappointed to learn I was leaving, but wanted the best for me and hoped this decision was within God's plan, not just my own. We agreed that I needed to continue my journey of getting to know God, but I didn't see why I couldn't do it at the U of I. The truth was I really wanted to get back with my high school friends and closer to home. Dave didn't think I'd made this decision for the right reasons and I knew in my gut he was right. However, I'd made up my mind. I was leaving.

When I realized Dave was not going to give up, I started edging my way toward the door. I didn't like the way this argument made me feel. I just wanted to get out of there. I put my hand on the doorknob ready to flee, when Dave got in my face and said, *"Rick, I know you are going to be successful in life! The question is . . . will you be successful in the world's eyes, or in God's eyes?"*

That stopped me in my tracks. What exactly was my goal? Had I made the decision to transfer for the purpose of being more successful in this world? Was it because I wanted to be with my old friends?

Did I really think this was going to make me a better person of faith? I wasn't sure.

That was the last thing Dave Larsen ever said to me. I never saw him again.

A New Scene

Somehow, I managed to get out of my commitments (apartment lease, tuition at NIU, etc.) in Dekalb and found living arrangements in Champaign. The latter fell into place easily in that two of my best friends from high school had an opening where they lived. It was in the basement of the McKinley Presbyterian Church, close to everything on campus. The church let nine guys live downstairs for seventy-five dollars a semester! The accommodations weren't great, but the price was right.

When I arrived at the University of Illinois in 1968, I found myself much closer to the cultural revolution of the late sixties. It was a time for students to be anti-establishment, self-interested, open, free, experimenting with drugs, exploring open sexuality, and anti-war. As a major university known worldwide, the U of I was more at the epicenter of the counterculture and it was impossible to ignore. It's amazing how different the culture was here versus the uniformity and accepted Biblical values of the 1950s and early sixties.

I lived on the fringe of the counterculture. I loved hard rock bands like The Doors, Cream, Janis Joplin, and Jimi Hendrix as well as the peace-loving, anti-establishment music of Carole King, Joan Baez, James Taylor, Bob Dylan, and The Plastic Ono Band. There were often protests against the Vietnam War on the Quad or around the alma mater statue. The National Guard was called in more than once to restore peace and calm the protests.

With this as a backdrop, I began to seriously question what I thought and believed. Was the Vietnam War just plain wrong? Was

America trying to help a violated and abused people, or were we trying to take over the world? Is democracy a good thing? Was it right to depose leaders of other countries and replace them with those who had values more like America's? Was communism as bad as the media made it sound? Was the Soviet Union trying to take over the world, causing us to try to stop its spread in places like Vietnam before it reached our borders? If our government was lying to us about Vietnam, what else were they lying to us about? Should we support our government, our country, or should we protest and try to tear it down because it's immoral and wrong? And if everything I had believed about America and the world truly was bogus, what does that mean about my faith in God?

Once one starts down this road of mistrust, there is no end to it. Finally, you're faced with just two options, and the one you take will change your life forever. The first option is attractive, easier, and seems to offer the most pleasure. That is to accept there really is no truth except in the eyes of the beholder. This means what we believe is based entirely on our own experiences and biases and what one believes to be true is no more right or wrong than what another believes to be true. "Truth" becomes relative to our base of knowledge and the only judge of truth is the outcome of polls—which truth do more people believe? In the end, truth becomes based on what our culture says about an issue. This is where it gets tough personally, because if I disagree with "the herd," I very well might not be accepted by my friends. I will likely be judged as narrow-minded and unthinking. It's human nature for people to earnestly want their beliefs confirmed, so there is tremendous pressure to believe what those around you believe.

The second option is to be your own person by examining carefully everything you see and believe. Take a serious look at the history of mankind over centuries and compare events, circumstances, and outcomes from the past to what you see and believe today. What can be learned and applied from history? What constants are there in life over the ages and what does that mean for today? What books, theories, and ideas have been proven consistently true over time? What makes logical sense in the big picture? What seems to be innately true? What does your gut tell you? And what tests out to work in your life consistently?

At NIU, I searched for truth without a lot of pressure from the outside. At the U of I, I was finding it much easier to follow the crowd, and putting God first is not generally what "the crowd" does. So, for about three years I tried to put God on hold. He wasn't very popular on campus. After all, God is the ultimate authority, so the many students and faculty rejecting authority of every kind were sure to reject our Creator. I experimented. I tried living my life without God. The methods of getting to know God that Dave Larsen taught me went by the wayside. Why did I need to know God anyway? None of my friends paid much attention to Him that I could see, and they were doing okay. In fact, they could do *anything they wanted.* That sounded like fun! And it didn't seem to matter. There were no lightning strikes, no immediate punishment, seemingly no downside. *If God matters, where is He?*

I tested my beliefs thoroughly those three years and made my faith so private no one could see it. I continued to believe I had accepted Christ as the Person who had paid the price for my disobedience, my sin, and therefore I was going to heaven when I died. I was a "Christian." Maybe that was enough. Almost everyone else seemed to believe it was.

There was really only one person I could talk to about my struggles inside during this time—Jeanene Flowers. I met Jeanene as soon as I set foot on campus, because she was dating my high school friend who got me into McKinley. I was attracted to her immediately, but had to bide my time until she and my friend broke up. Then, I didn't waste any time. We've been together ever since.

Jeanene was not only beautiful, but thoughtful, wise, calm, caring, and a great decision-maker. She was (and is) a great friend to try things out on and I filled her ear with questions. Of course, she couldn't tell me what to think, but was a patient and loving listener as I sought to understand my faith.

Jeanene's hometown of Bellaire, Ohio was a small industrial town that had seen its better days. While she was growing up, her father managed soft drink bottling plants and moved from city to city every few years for promotions or a better job. When Jeanene was in high school, they moved to Aurora, Illinois. Without this turn of events, the University of Illinois would never have been on her radar screen of school choices. She was an Ohio girl at heart. But now, the U of I was the best school for her.

My decision to transfer schools might have been made for the wrong reasons, but God didn't give up on me just because I made a bad choice. I may have disappointed Him, but He remained steadfast in guiding me toward my best life. Because, meeting Jeanene was the best thing that ever happened to me.

Job Hunting

Upon graduation, my first choice was to find a job in Champaign. I interviewed with a few local companies, although I had few connections. Nothing looked promising, but I did have one good interview. My brother Larry knew Rick Springer, who was a VP at Research Press, a small educational publishing company just started in 1968. They didn't have an opening, but I didn't forget about it.

In January of 1971, I moved to Berwyn, a suburb of Chicago, to live with Joanne and Tom and look for work in the big city. I had lived there the past two summers to make enough money to pay for the next year of college. I had nothing left over to live on and student loans to pay, so I went back to work at an old summer job in a distribution facility, while also going on interviews for a "real job" to get my business career started.

The summer job I went back to was at Goldblatt's warehouse. My supervisor (Henry) in the mattress department was a really good man. The warehouse was located in a tough part of the city and the workforce reflected that. Henry knew the only other young guy and I weren't permanent, but we worked harder than everyone else and he appreciated that. I got pretty good at driving a forklift truck to move pallets of mattresses from trucks to racks thirty feet in the air, which came in handy later.

At break time, most everyone went across the street to a neighborhood bar for a shot and a beer. Lunchtime, too. Then, back onto the forklift truck—not exactly the safest thing to do, but no one seemed to mind. Clearly this was not a career job for me, but it was for most everyone else there.

This might have seemed to be an inconsequential stop along my journey, but God doesn't waste any of our time on Earth. Goldblatt's became another key turning point for me. The experience helped me understand how different life is for socio-economic groups other than my own. A life lived with a family unable to support you, in a high-rise apartment building or small, zero-lot-line house in a big city, with a different ethnicity, no money, little opportunity, or without U.S. citizenship causes one to view life very differently. All the assumptions that make decisions seem so logical to me must be discarded before I can begin to understand why another makes the decisions he or she makes. Expecting others to make decisions based on my own assumptions is a fool's game. Like never before, at Goldblatt's I learned to respect every person equally, regardless of color, status, beliefs, or anything else. This foundational truth became very important to the success I would experience later in life.

It also gave me time to think again about everything I'd learned over the previous years, from Nelda's death to living life with, then without, God. As I wrestled with this, I believe the Holy Spirit showed up. There was no mentor or friend by my side now to help me figure it out, and the environment I worked in provided little guidance. But, I felt a nudge to find out more.

Without any plan in mind, I started going to sit in my '67 Barracuda at break and lunch times to read the Bible instead of going to the neighborhood bar for a shot and a beer. I pulled out a Phillips translation of the New Testament that I'd studied with Dave Larsen and began reading and praying. After three years of putting Him on the back burner, I felt God put a stirring in my heart. I found He had never left me alone, even though I'd done my best to ignore Him! I was ready now to return to my journey with God.

Amazingly, miraculously, but not surprisingly, it was just at this time the breakthrough that started my career came to pass. None of my many interviews in Chicago had panned out, but once every few weeks I would call Rick Springer at Research Press to see if any kind of job had opened up there. Finally, my persistence paid off. He said they had a Warehouse Manager's position open, but it was a small warehouse with only the manager and one part-time worker—certainly below my credentials. I said, "I'll take it!" I knew in my gut there was something right about this company.

There was.

2

Priorities

Research Press (RP) was about three years old when I started in 1971. There were less than twenty people in the little publishing company and the owner was a book salesman turned publisher.

On my first day, I saw all kinds of things that could be done better—in the office as well as the warehouse—and I started doing them. I think it made Bob Parkinson, the owner, realize administration was not his strong suit and he was better able to do what he did best with me handling operations. He encouraged me to keep making changes and, within two weeks, named me Operations Manager.

This is when I first learned that responsibility is not so much given as it is earned. Owners want their businesses to succeed, of course. That's why simply doing whatever I could do to make that happen for Bob worked out well for me. I took on greater and greater responsibility as I saw needs. I asked a lot of hard questions, which allowed me to learn the publishing business quickly. Within three months Rick Springer (who had hired me) resigned, leaving even more holes for me to fill. All this was confirmation to me that God was at work in giving me this opportunity at RP.

When first offered the position, I felt like my life had turned a corner and it was already proving to be true. I loved what I was doing and was beginning to meet peers who would become lifelong friends.

Life was taking shape and I wanted Jeanene to be a part of it from the beginning. I believed I was on the right path and wanted Jeanene Flowers to go on this life journey with me.

My proposal was not the most romantic and a long way from the productions they are today. After driving across town one day, we arrived at our destination and parked at a curb. I turned off my Barracuda and, looking forward through the windshield with the gearshift and console between us, I said, "I think the timing is right, Jeanene—we should get married." It was an anemic effort, but, thankfully, she said, "Yes!"

Growth Steps through Mentors

Jeanene and I were married on February 26, 1972, about four months after I started at RP. I was filled with confidence, because this big piece of my life's puzzle had fallen into place. Jeanene was the right girl for me. She would make me be a better person.

She wasn't so sure I'd do the same for her. I didn't know what was going through her mind on our wedding day, but she looked like she might turn and run. (It's obvious in our wedding photos.) Fortunately for me, she decided to take the plunge and, after we sealed the deal at the church, she didn't look back.

We began our married life living in government-subsidized housing in Champaign, Illinois, thanks to our ultra-low income. We lived in a newly built apartment complex outside of town and it was a great price—another blessing from God, because it helped us pay down our school loans.

Before moving to Champaign, I prayed I would meet someone like Dave Larsen who would help me grow in my faith. I knew I couldn't do it alone. One day I heard a few people were getting together to try to revive the YFC (Youth for Christ) ministry in Champaign-Urbana.

Cru and the Navigators certainly had made a difference in my life, so I was partial to para-church organizations. I decided to attend.

At the meeting, I met David Gardner, then Professor of Marketing at the U of I. Dave was about ten years older than I, a handsome man, even though I thought he dressed a little frumpy—a typical professor look. I caught his eye during the meeting and afterwards he came over to introduce himself. He said, "You asked some really good questions there. How about joining me and a few others each week to pray for Youth for Christ?" I didn't know it at the time, but Dave was the answer to my prayer—a spiritual mentor. I began to pray weekly in a small group of four people.

Two things stood out to me during this time. First was the generosity of one of the men in our prayer group. There was a small amount of funding from the community for YFC, but money was always scarce. Our one staff person received very little compensation, but she worked hard to share the love of Christ with junior high and high school kids and never complained. I remember spotting this businessman secretly giving her hundred-dollar bills on the side. Giving that much money away, freely and without fanfare, caught my attention. I also remember wondering how anyone could have that much cash in his pockets!

The other thing that stuck with me was the strong belief in prayer these people had. They met every single week, believing the only way YFC would grow strong was through prayer. It would be by God's hand, and no one else's. We met for over two years to pray for YFC. That ministry is still going strong in the Champaign-Urbana area today, and Jeanene and I have supported it financially for almost fifty years, largely inspired by this prayer group and its generosity many years ago.

Dave Gardner became my friend, mentor, and close advisor over the course of my business career. When our YFC prayer group ended,

Dave and I continued to meet in Hessel Park each week, early in the morning, to pray for our work, our family, and our community. Dave taught me how to pray.

A few years after joining the YFC prayer group, I met another man who greatly impacted my life. This man taught me the Word of God. Bill Edwards was a former U of I basketball player who had become very successful in the insurance business. His athletic and business success gave him a large sphere of influence, which he used to demonstrate God's love in our community.

I had never seen such a successful person who was willing to put his faith first like Bill did. It was so unusual for someone who seemed to already "have it all" take the risk of putting faith first. In my experience, successful people tended to hide their faith, not wanting to offend a potential client or customer. It was okay—even a good thing—to believe in God, but faith had its place and it wasn't in business, according to this mindset. Letting people know you believed Jesus is the Savior for everyone in the world was a limb simply too high to climb for most. But Bill didn't subscribe to this theory. God was a part of everything he did, and he let everyone know it.

Bill started a men's Bible Study Fellowship (BSF) group in Champaign. I had met him before, but didn't think he knew me from Adam. So, when he approached me one day and asked me personally to join the introductory BSF class, I jumped at the chance! I loved being around successful people. After the introductory class, BSF became a mainstay in Champaign-Urbana. I soon became a discussion leader and studied the Old and New Testament like it was a college course for the next twenty years.

BSF met weekly, and every city across the country with a BSF class was on the same schedule. It was and is to this day a structured program and few misses were allowed. Discussion leaders met Saturday morning for two hours to prepare for leading their small groups the next Monday evening. If a discussion leader missed Saturday, he was unable to lead his group Monday. I didn't like missing my Monday group, so, when traveling for work (which I did a lot), I would sometimes drive a hundred miles one way to attend the nearest BSF Leader's Meeting. It was worth it.

BSF was the best method for me to get to know God, and to put faith first, as I saw Bill do. The more I learned to apply the Bible to my life, the more I saw how God played a part in everything I was doing. Between Dave Gardner teaching me how to pray and Bill Edwards teaching me the Bible, God had certainly answered my request to find people in Champaign-Urbana who would help me grow in faith.

Life Lessons Learned

During these years of mentoring and being mentored, I was also learning the educational publishing business. In the beginning it was more about budgeting, operations, marketing, working with banks to maintain the cash flow needed to grow the business, and the like—the business side of things. But, God had more in mind for me to learn at Research Press (RP) that would prepare me well for the future.

RP published educational material based on behavioral psychology. Our books were used in mental health centers, college courses, and counseling/treatment centers for those with disabilities. Occasionally, a book would bleed over into a larger market. *Living with Children* by Gerald R. Patterson was one of those books and the book that spearheaded RP's success.

What all our books proposed was that learning can be much more effective when the child, student, or person involved is positively reinforced and encouraged for doing something right, and ignored or redirected when their behavior is unacceptable. This concept falls within the realm of what is called "behavioral psychology."

The father of behavioral psychology is B.F. Skinner, a controversial social scientist at Harvard. As we grew and became better known in the industry, we had the opportunity to make a documentary with Dr. Skinner. I was certainly in the background of this project, but our filmmaker from California and Dr. Skinner had a rocky relationship that sometimes needed to be dealt with. I was as nervous as could be, but one day I called Dr. Skinner at his Harvard office to try to straighten things out.

To my surprise, Dr. Skinner himself answered the phone on the second ring. "Dr. Skinner?" I stammered. Adrenaline shot through me in a wave. *What can I say now to sound halfway intelligent?* I was only in my twenties and far from being a scientist. "This is Rick Stephens from Research Press, and I just wanted to reach out concerning the film we're making with you. I understand your recent interaction with Mr. Blake was less than ideal, so I wanted to see if I can answer any questions you may have . . ."

Dr. Skinner was happy to know we cared enough to call him and work it out. I couldn't believe it, but that was all it took. He was kind enough to put me at ease and we had a very friendly conversation about the issues at hand. Communication solves so many problems. My natural tendency was always to shy away from conflict, but whenever I met it head-on, all the wrong assumptions made on both sides could be discussed and cleared up. Without communication, the wrong assumptions just multiply.

God was actively involved in my life during this pivotal stage of development in so many ways. He led me to Dave Gardner and Bill Edwards, to my YFC prayer group and BSF. Jeanene and I met lifelong friends while at RP, and I learned how to run a business. I came to understand that leading people by reinforcing them for doing things right and redirecting bad choices is empowering (and it works!). I learned the best way to interact with people, noteworthy (like a B.F. Skinner) or not, is by being genuine. And through the books we published, Jeanene and I were given a heart for those with disabilities. This passion was instrumental in decisions we made later.

When Fear Takes Hold

Bob Parkinson, the owner of RP, had a heart attack in 1976 and it scared him, compelling him to re-evaluate his life's priorities and retire to Florida. He left the company mostly in my hands—naming me president as soon as he recovered from heart bypass surgery and moved away. We talked on the phone often, but he only visited Champaign once or twice a year. What an opportunity for an ambitious twenty-eight-year-old! I thought, "It's pretty amazing that God kept me thinking about RP while looking for my first career job. I've gone from Warehouse Manager to President within five years!" Life was good.

RP grew significantly the next few years. The longer I was President, the more confident I became making strategic decisions for its future. I believed behavioral technology would work just as well in the business environment as it did for children and those with disabilities. We began publishing authors who were applying behavioral science successfully in management, leadership, and business. This broadened our market considerably, which led to even more growth.

However, Bob did not feel as comfortable outside the educational marketplace. He and I began to butt heads as I took more risks. My vision was to grow the company in order to share this positive and effective method of leadership with many more people. His vision was to stick with what he knew and not take any big risks. He lived a comfortable life with his wife in Del Ray Beach, Florida and didn't want to jeopardize his income stream.

Our relationship became more difficult in 1979-80, about eight years after I started at RP. I became troubled and sought God's direction during this time. I remember asking God to clear up the misunderstandings and help Bob and me get on the same track. I'd end my prayer with, "Yet . . . Your will be done, not my own."

I didn't get the answer I wanted. I started feeling in my gut that it was time to move on, but I was afraid to leave. I depended on that paycheck and was afraid I'd never be able to replace my salary, especially staying in Champaign. I thought to myself, *What would people think if I left without another good job lined up?* I was in Rotary Club and the Champaign Country Club, and was viewed as an "up and comer" in the community. I was not willing to risk losing it all.

And so . . . I stayed. Fear of taking a risk—despite a gut feeling from God—and small-minded thinking were not qualities I was proud of, but it was just too scary. I soon learned that not following God's lead carries far greater risk than taking a step into the unknown with Him.

By late 1980, things had become very tense between Bob and me and it was time for his annual visit. I didn't know what to expect. I'd procrastinated for two years, playing it safe by hanging on, ignoring God's whispers to step out in faith. That wasn't working very well, so I was prepared for whatever Bob had to say to me on this visit. At least, I thought I was.

When he arrived at RP, he made a bee line for my office. He was a big, round man and frankly, not in great shape. My office was all the way at the end of the hall, so he was huffing and puffing by the time he got to me. He sat down, took a few deep breaths and looked me square in the eye. "It's time for you to leave Research Press, Rick." And that was that.

I sat, dumbfounded. Bob kept talking but I didn't hear what he said. I was in a daze. Finally, I snapped out of it and could tell this was really hard for him, too. I had become like a son to him. I opened my mouth and questions poured out. "But the company is growing and showing better profits. Who else would you have lead? What about all the people that have come to depend on me? What will you say to them? What about the authors I have good relationships with?" Obviously, I had come to believe I was a lot more important than I actually was.

Bob continued to breathe heavily and I didn't want him to have another heart attack, so I stopped asking questions and he left my office. I didn't know what to do next, how to act. Everything was blurred. I sat staring at the wall for what seemed like an eternity. Finally, I got up and left without saying a word to anyone. That was the last time I was ever in the RP building while people were there. No goodbyes. No well wishes. No going away party. I just left.

Later in life I realized that what I'd done was to become my usual mode of operation (MO). I could have left RP long before I got fired—any time during those last two years when I knew in my heart it was time to move on. But, fear of the unknown locked me in place, and I waited until I was forced out. Then, I slithered out secretly to avoid making anyone feel uncomfortable, including myself.

For some peculiar reason, I have a hard time taking credit for accomplishments and moving on with my head held high. I'm better just leaving in the quiet of the night. A longtime basketball fan, I loved the Chicago Bulls when Michael Jordan, Scottie Pippen, and Dennis Rodman won all those championships. My hero in that group was Rodman. He rebounded the ball so well and made the outlet pass. Wow! Jordan and Pippen scored all the points, but Rodman set the plate for them to be successful. That was the MO I wanted to be known for. To build the structure, set the plate, create the environment necessary for success, but let others shine. I wanted to win the championship, but didn't want all eyes on me.

Picking up the Pieces

I went straight home after being fired. Jeanene was running errands with our three girls (Jill was five, Carrie three, and Marnie three months). When she came home and saw me, she knew something was terribly wrong. I worked long hours and was never home during the day.

I was broken, humiliated, and depressed. "Bob just fired me and I don't know what to do," I said. She put her things away, got the kids settled, and just held me. We were both devastated and worried.

This was our first big test as a couple and Jeanene demonstrated what a courageous, solid, and faithful partner God had given me. I probably would have folded without Jeanene by my side. She is the strong one, not me. Whatever I have accomplished in life, I assure you, would not have occurred without her in my life. She brings out the best in me.

In the aftermath I spent a lot of time crying out to God. I prayed, "Oh Lord, I've tried to follow You. I go to Bible Study Fellowship two times a week. I'm a discussion leader. I've spoken out for You in public. I have a quiet time almost every day. We go to church and give money to Your causes. How could You let this happen?"

I thought that since my boxes were checked, I was immune to trials. *What are people going to think? How will I ever be able to replace my salary? Will people think I performed poorly at my job? Who will hire me? How will I feed my family?* On and on. I spiraled deeper and deeper into depression.

It was embarrassing to go out in public. I "knew" people were talking about me. (Actually, they probably had their own issues and didn't care much about mine, but that's not how I saw it.) It was hard to tell people I was out of work. I tried to not blame it all on Bob, because I knew it never worked to say bad things about your former boss, but I must admit that I was not fond of him at the time. I thought I was doing a great job for RP.

Regardless of what anyone thought, the fact remained I needed a job. With a wife, baby, toddler, and preschooler, it was not a choice. I could either continue to feel sorry for myself or buck it up and get myself out there. Jeanene sealed it when she said, "Stop feeling sorry for yourself, Rick, because it doesn't do any good. You need to think that right now, finding a new job is . . . your new job!"

She was right. I was in a new stage now; it was time to take it seriously.

God Has a Plan

I went to the library searching books and articles on how best to find a job. (Today, of course, all we'd have to do is Google it.) I followed their direction by listing my strengths and weaknesses, what I enjoyed doing most in my old job, and what duties I enjoyed least. I defined my "ideal role" in a company and what kind of company I wanted to work in, wrote a resume using models from the books, studied how to prepare for an interview, and made a list of companies to pursue. Then I went after it.

Jeanene is convinced I worked harder when looking for a job than I did when I had a job. I used every contact I had to get interviews, talked with anyone who would talk to me, and gave it all I had, because I needed to find something *soon*. I was afraid it would take months to find a decent job and it would probably require moving, but, as usual, God had something in mind. He was just waiting until I left RP. Since I didn't have the courage, He made the decision for me.

One day a friend mentioned that one of the partners at Great Planes Model Distributors (GP) had just left. "Apparently the two weren't getting along. Maybe the remaining partner would want to replace him," my source told me. He made a call for me and I got an interview. I researched the company and tried to figure out what I might be able to contribute before talking with them. Then I went to an interview with the owner, Don Anderson.

Don was an engineer and had started this company in conjunction with his college roommate, Bruce Holecek. Bruce started Tower Hobbies while a student at the U of I and had achieved astonishing success. Later he encouraged Don to start a distribution company and Tower Hobbies would be his biggest customer. Don did so, bringing Eric Meyers in as a fifty-fifty partner in the company. After seven years they were at odds and the only way out was for one to sell to the other. Don borrowed the money to buy Eric's share and Eric left GP.

This happened one month before I was fired at RP. *One month!* Just the right amount of time for Don to grasp his new situation and start looking for a replacement. I believed I was the man for the job.

Don had a hard time visualizing me in his company. Eric was a well-known expert modeler widely respected in the radio control hobby industry. He understood the product and marketplace like no one else. He was a special talent.

My task was to convince Don the reason he and Eric had trouble was because they both were modelers and both understood the product, but had strong (differing) opinions about how to sell it. I said, "I know nothing about the product, so you won't have that problem with me. But, I do know how to run a business. Let me run the business side of things, and you can focus on the product, which is what you really enjoy."

I did my best to convince Don I could contribute to GP. It wasn't an easy sell. He continued to struggle with the fact I knew nothing about remote control (R/C) airplanes, so I finally said, "Just give it a try for a few months. If it doesn't work out, we'll both know, and I'll leave without any pain. No harm, no foul." And with that, he agreed.

Miraculously, I had found a job within two weeks of leaving RP, at the same salary, in the same Champaign/Urbana area. I had been too afraid to leave RP, because I didn't trust God and I let fear win out. But God wouldn't give up on me. He forced the issue when I wouldn't, and then showed me He had already taken care of the things I feared.

This was a lesson I will never forget. Now, when I know the right thing to do and feel it in my gut, I don't hesitate. It likely means God is calling me to follow His plan instead of my own. What He has in mind will be far better for me than "playing it safe," and choosing to *not* follow His lead will cost dearly in lost adventures and blessings that might have been.

3

Leading from Behind

Great Planes was a humbling experience for me. At RP, I was president. I understood the business, could make my own decisions, and loved that the buck stopped with me. I was important! At GP, I was a novice in a new industry—nothing more than an assistant to the president—and all the important decisions were made by him. I was a leader, a driver, predisposed to "make things happen." I never felt comfortable in the back seat and that's where I sat at Great Planes. Little did I know there was so much in store for me to learn the next five years about leadership and about myself.

Despite my lack of enthusiasm about my position, I had a job to do, so I tried to ignore the "step-down" and contribute wherever I could to GP's success. My background allowed me to identify ways we could do things better and devise plans that would improve efficiency and profits, just like I had done at RP. Don recognized the contribution I was making, and our mutual respect grew quickly.

More than anything, Don loved designing radio control (RC) airplanes and setting up the facilities to manufacture them efficiently. And he was good at it. He was creative and smart. As he learned to trust me with the operations of the business, he began to focus his energy on the design and development of new products. During my first two years with him, he bought several manufacturing companies and combined them to form Great Planes Manufacturing. Since Don spent most of his time on the manufacturing end of things, I was able to make most decisions for GP Distributors. This gave me a chance to really learn the hobby business. But, for some reason, I was not truly happy at GP. It felt like a temporary stop.

The future became a little more uncertain when Don told me his former partner wanted to return to the company. Eric Meyers had traveled for two years after leaving GP, but he loved the hobby industry and missed being a part of it. He wanted to come back to GP and Don wanted him back, too. This, of course, was very threatening to me, because it was quite possible it would leave me without a job yet again. But, after interviewing him, God gave me a peace that I did not expect. Eric clearly had a lot to offer and the company would be more successful with him in it, so we hired him. He reported to me.

We now had a really good team at GP Distributors. Don was designing, developing, and producing high-quality models in GP Manufacturing. Eric was marketing our products extremely well, Janet Ottmers and Debra Love were building a professional sales team, and we had a great group of employees who were making day-to-day operations run smoothly. Don made all the important decisions for the company, but he gave me the freedom to manage most things related to GP Distributors on my own.

I began to lead GP as if it were my company as much as I could. I scheduled a time for strategic planning, which Don was skeptical about at first. He knew what he was doing and just wanted to get on with it. Spending valuable time talking about it wasn't his cup of tea, but to his credit he allowed me to move forward.

At these planning sessions I would lead our entire group of managers in discussions about *why* we were doing what we were doing, *what* exactly was our mission, and *how* to best accomplish it. It gave everyone a chance to give input and help decide key objectives for the near future. Don participated and I think found them to be helpful.

When our largest customer (Tower Hobbies, of course) was rattling our cage because we had raised our price to them, I saw another opportunity to take on more responsibility. Don still had the relationship with Tower because of the history between Don and Bruce, but he was tired of the constant headaches he had to deal with. I suggested that I could relieve his frustrations if I became the primary contact with Tower. He was concerned, because I didn't have his product knowledge and we couldn't afford to lose those sales. However, he decided to give me a shot at it.

Tower wasn't happy about this and tried to go around me, as expected, but Don was great—he didn't interfere. I began to establish a good working relationship with the folks at Tower, which allowed Don the freedom to do things that were more important to the company's success. They were also things he enjoyed more.

As at RP before, I persistently pushed to gain more authority and it paid off for me and the company. I remember more than once telling Don, "I want the job you're doing, so you can do new things no one has time for now that will take the company to a new level." Intrapreneurship is when an employee acts like an entrepreneur within a company. Intrapreneurs are self-motivated, proactive people who take the initiative to do whatever needs to be done for the company to succeed. That was me, and it was the type of people I yearned for later on when I had my own company.

At GP I wasn't president, and I wasn't in the role I wanted to be in, but it was the job I had. Colossians 3:23 says, "Whatever you do, work at it with all your heart, as working for the Lord, not for human masters." As long as I was at GP, I wanted to do my job as if I owned the company and was working directly for God. That meant doing my very best to make the company successful.

Don was right to be concerned about my ability to manage the Tower relationship. It was a challenge. Tower Hobbies made up over 50 percent of our revenues, but at a very low gross margin. We needed to ramp up our sales to hobby shops to increase our margin and lessen our dependence on one customer while continuing to grow our overall sales.

Tower expected a very low price from GP due to their high volume and hobby shops were skeptical of GP because they knew we sold a lot to Tower. Store owners didn't like any mail order companies that discounted heavily, and Tower was the largest one of all. Hobby shops believed Tower had an unfair advantage, because it could buy cheaper due to its volume and didn't have to charge sales tax as a national retailer shipping out of state. For many hobby shops, buying from GP was like buying from their biggest competitor.

However, I knew we had one thing going for us and that was our extraordinary service levels. Eric's marketing knowledge showed hobby shops how to sell more product. Our sales team was caring, sensitive, and responsive to shops. We had all the products shops needed, when they needed it, and we got it to them in one to three days. It was hard for shops to ignore us, because we made it easier and more profitable for them in the long run. Slowly we moved our ratio of sales to 85 percent hobby shops, 15 percent Tower, while continuing to grow overall sales.

The Tides Turn

This wasn't working well for Tower, however, so its owner, Bruce, tried to buy GP in an effort to turn the tides back in his favor. But Don didn't want to work for Bruce.

Then, in 1984, a well-respected and visionary businessman in Champaign became involved. His name was Clint Atkins. Clint was a tall, blond, good-looking guy with a down-home style. He was a tough businessman, but his loyalty and generosity to those he liked and trusted was legendary. He also was a good citizen, using his resources freely to improve our community.

Clint had made a fortune in the apartment and property development business. He wanted to diversify, so he approached Bruce to buy Tower Hobbies. Clint thought like a true entrepreneur. Rather than bicker and negotiate with Bruce to get Tower at the lowest possible price, he looked not at what Tower was worth on paper, but what he could make from owning it.

Clint offered Bruce a compelling amount of cash, full authority to continue to run the company, all the capital he needed to grow it, and 50 percent of the profits from then on. It was an offer that Bruce did not refuse. Clint figured that Bruce's keen business acumen in the hobby industry would give him a great return on his investment. And he was right.

Over the next thirty years, he made back his investment many times over and eventually sold the company for a huge multiple of his initial investment. I had always admired Clint as a shrewd businessman, but this was the first time I had a front row seat to dealings like this. In fact, I was fascinated. I learned a lot from Clint about buying businesses that was very helpful in my own business down the road.

Unfortunately for me and my team, Clint's strategy also included buying GP. Owning both GP and Tower would allow him to eliminate the wholesaler margin and increase their pricing advantage over competitors. Immediately after buying Tower, Clint approached Don and he had his ear.

In like manner, Clint offered Don significant cash, as well as the promise of a high-paying job he would enjoy for life. At the time, I was one of Don's advisors, so we talked freely about the decision for several months. I knew a sale would put my job in serious jeopardy but, knowing Don the way I did, I had to advise him to sell. Clint correctly judged what was important to Don and made an offer that met all his needs.

One day, Don asked me to ride with him to his hometown: Paris, Illinois. He was still chewing on the offer and wanted to talk to his father, a conservative farmer. It was a compelling number and his dad said, "That's a lot of money, son. I'd take it and run." On the ride back home it dawned on me that this was probably going to happen. My career was headed for a jolt. I thought, *I don't know what God has planned for me in this, but He is in control and it will be okay.* This attitude gave me a sense of peace that turned what could have been a very stressful situation into an interesting adventure.

Don accepted the offer and the deal closed in December, 1984. Don became the Vice President of Manufacturing for the combined companies (Tower and GP) and I became President of GP Distributors.

GP Distributors was now my responsibility and we had a nearly impossible task ahead of us. We were expected to maintain our sales to hobby shops, feed product to Tower at very little markup, and increase bottom line profit. How could we maintain our sales to hobby shops when it was public knowledge we were owned by their arch enemy? And how could we increase profits when a huge percentage of our sales were intercompany at low margin?

However, our team met the mission with tenacity. We were able to build a workable strategy and went after it. Our message to the stores was, "I know it's hard to grasp, but this can actually work *for* you. You'll still receive the great service you've come to expect from GP, and now Tower has a built-in incentive to not discount their prices so much. This will give you a better chance to compete with mail order than ever before." It was a tough sell, but our customers wanted to believe us and it worked.

I figured if I did a great job as President of GP, I had a good chance of becoming president of the combined companies (now called Hobbico). It would be my dream job and an outstanding outcome after all the uncertainty. Clint had told me Bruce was essentially retiring and moving to Florida. This was confirmed when they began a search for someone to run the new company in his absence. I would have the freedom to do something special if I were leader of Hobbico.

I remember speaking to a friend of mine—a colleague who had worked for Bruce for years—who was also a believer. "Alan," I said, "I can't say this to anyone else, but I know you'll understand. It seems like everything has fallen into place so miraculously in the past year. Clint becoming involved, buying these two companies, putting them together, and naming me President of GP. I think God is paving the way for me to become President of Hobbico!" I even quoted Psalm 118:23 to him: "The Lord has done this and it is marvelous in our eyes."

Alan's reaction was subdued, which seemed a little odd. I put this in the back of my mind, but wanted to believe I was the guy and God was going to make it happen in spite of what Alan thought. Later I learned that he was in the inner circle with Bruce and Clint and knew the likelihood of my becoming president was very slim. But, I didn't know it at the time, so I trucked on.

I prayed earnestly and believed this was in fact what God had in mind. I continued to claim Psalm 118:23. In my morning quiet times with God, I reviewed with Him all that He had done in my career to prepare me for just this job. I reminded Him how He had led me to RP, allowed me to be promoted to president, led me away from RP, miraculously prepared a top opening for me at Great Planes, allowed me to learn a new industry, permitted me to become trusted in the field, and just at the right time, brought these two companies together. He did this to create the perfect job for me. It sure seemed like this was God's plan.

But . . . I was wrong. I didn't realize it then, but God was actually preparing me for something much bigger and better.

One day in late April of 1985, Bruce wanted to talk to me. He and I had very little contact, so this was out of the ordinary. I felt strangely peaceful that he had chosen a Sunday morning to meet with me, during the time I normally attended church. For some reason it made me think God was going with me. I believed I was about to be told that everything I had been praying and hoping for was going to come to pass.

When I got there, I realized it was only the two of us in the building. I was expecting to see Clint, since this was such a big decision. Bruce got right to the point, telling me that he, not Clint, was the one to decide who would be the president of Hobbico, because, in fact, he intended to remain very much involved. I could see Clint was relying on Bruce to continue to run his hobby companies—remotely. What Bruce needed was someone to be his eyes and ears at Hobbico and do his bidding. He wasn't looking for someone like me. I not only didn't get the job I wanted, I was fired. Again.

I went home that Sunday morning to, once again, tell Jeanene I'd been fired. I remained surprisingly calm and was relieved to find out she felt the same sense of peace about our situation. Not that we weren't worried, because we were! But we also believed God had His hand all over this, just as in other critical times of our life. He had taken care of us so far, and we were confident He would again. We were comforted by this as we sat facing each other in our kitchen, without a job or any stream of income and three young children.

This was a wake-up call for me. After getting canned for the second time in five years, I realized that I had been imposing my own thoughts and goals onto God. I had been coaching Him, as if He needed help in providing for my life! I had been focusing on the smaller picture in front of me, thinking I could see what God's plan was and I needed to make it happen. But now, I believed God had a much bigger picture in mind all along, and He certainly didn't need my help in deciding how to paint that picture.

This is one of the many incidents through which Jeanene and I learned to look for the big picture in all aspects of our life, including when facing disappointment and failure. Bad things happen to people. Job loss, illness, death, divorce, financial loss, addiction, and more are all part of life on Earth. While in the muck, it was difficult for us to see beyond the problems, but we had come through them before and life turned out to be okay on the other side, (usually even better!).

God had shown us that He was in control. In our kitchen that night, we had a strange sense of anticipation that this time, we were on the cusp of something really big.

4

The Promised Land

My severance package from GP included two months' pay, which meant I had something to get us through May and June of that year. We didn't even have enough savings to get us through July. I needed to be working by July 1st. Nothing like a little pressure, right?

Jeanene and I never lived beyond our means, but in our younger stages of life, we struggled to build emergency funds. It's hard to save money when you have a young family and are still building your career. We knew we didn't have much time, but we decided to use what time we had to look for a way to get into my *own* business. Jeanene was kidding (but not kidding) when she told her friends, "Rick needs a company of his own, because it may be the only way he can ever hold a job!"

There was a lot of truth in that statement, because I had my own vision for what RP should become, and my own vision for Great Planes/Hobbico, too. In my opinion, they were ambitious, exciting strategies based on good business sense and Christian principles, which I thought worked really well together. However, in both cases, my vision was different than the owner's vision. If I wanted to cast my vision for a company, I needed to be the owner.

My Own Vision

I began looking for an existing company to buy or an idea to start a company. Since we had no money to invest, I would also have to find a way to finance it. For example, maybe I could find a company with an owner wanting to bring in a protégé to learn the business so he or she could retire. Or, maybe I could find an angel investor or equity partner to provide the money while I provided the idea and sweat equity. I was eager and ready.

My first idea was to start a company like Great Planes had been before the acquisition. I was convinced hobby shops would not be served well by Hobbico. Hobbico's vision was to produce more profit through Tower Hobbies, because that's where the largest margin was. It would likely be harder than ever for hobby shops to buy from GP if Hobbico's focus was primarily on the Tower division.

I drafted a business plan that showed I had a solid chance of survival if I could sell as little as two million in product the first year. To achieve some penetration into the market, our gross margin would likely be low—in the 15 percent range. That would give us $300,000 to work with. We could hire a few people, get a small warehouse, convince some manufacturers to sell to us, and give stores another source of supply. It might never become very large, but—hey!—it would give me and some others a job.

The plan made sense except for three major problems:

1. I had no capital to start a company.
2. Hobbico had seemingly unlimited capital, which they could use to force me out of business in a short time through cutthroat pricing, if they chose to.
3. Clint and Bruce would not be happy with me. They would likely use their considerable influence locally and in the industry to keep me from starting or succeeding.

It was just too big of a risk, so I pursued other options. I looked at every possibility I could uncover that my experience in publishing and distribution might have prepared me for, including office supply distribution, plumbing supplies, contractor supplies, musical instruments, software delivery, and more. I tested the waters to see if RP might be for sale, now five years after my departure. No chance. I talked with anyone who would talk to me about an idea that would lead me to having my own company. Nothing panned out.

By the end of June, the matter was becoming serious. Clint offered me a job as president of a craft distribution company he had recently purchased (Herr's), but there was little future in that job. I would have had very little authority, because I now knew Bruce was his man in the hobby industry. However, unless something better materialized soon, I would have to take it. It was the safe option.

God's Best

Jeanene and I kept asking God to show us what He had in mind. His answer seemed to be, *Start a hobby company like GP. Yes, it's dangerous but I am with you; you can do all things through Me.*[1]

We were both studying Genesis in BSF at the time and we were struck by Genesis 12:1-5. In this passage, God tells Abram to leave Haran, the land he knew, and go to a new land—the land of Canaan, which he knew nothing about. Abram, at age seventy-five (or so), got up and went. Just like that!

Abram was a wealthy guy, well-known, respected, and comfortable in life. He had wives, sons, livestock, servants, tents, and money. He had a great life. But God said, "Go from your country, your people

---

1. Philippians 4:13

and your father's household to the land I will show you. I will make you into a great nation, and I will bless you . . . and all peoples on Earth will be blessed through you."

That's a big ask, don't you think? Leave what you know. Leave a very good life. Leave your people, your connections, your history, and go to this place you've never been. Risk everything for an unknown land. How would you react, if that was asked of you? Most people would settle for the good life they already knew, even if the unknown land might be grander. Any business advisor would agree that it just wasn't worth the risk. Unless . . . that advisor knew God!

God would later call this Promised Land "a land flowing with milk and honey" (Deuteronomy 26:8-9). He was telling Abram that though his life was *good* in Haran, it was not God's *best*. By saying, "Yes," Abram went on to experience an adventure with God that changed the world.

It gives me chills today to think about how clear this analogy was in my own life. I could've taken the job at Herr's. It was the safe play—paychecks would've been consistent and more than I made before. It would have been a very good life. But, we felt God was telling us, *Get up, leave the safety of this life you know, and I will take you on an adventure of a lifetime.*

Soon God made the pathway a little clearer. Miraculously, the people I needed to start the company—my core team at GP—were suddenly available and wanting to start a new company with me. Eric, Debra, and Janet were the trio I'd worked closely with at GP and, by July 3rd, all three had called me to say they had either been fired or were going to leave. These were the people I needed—Eric for product knowledge, purchasing, and marketing, Debra for inside sales, and Janet for outside sales. I could do everything else, but needed these specialists to fill my big weak spots. And now, they were all available and encouraging me to start the company.

Taking this kind of risk was way outside my conservative nature. I definitely would have taken the safe route except that I felt in my gut God was saying, *Get up and go,* and Jeanene agreed. Going against the guidance of those two was a non-starter.

On July 4th, I crossed the line. I said to Jeanene, "Let's go for it. Let's start this new company and see where God leads us. And I think we should call it Horizon Hobby because it's a new beginning, like the dawning of a new day." She lit up with excitement. She had known it was the right thing to do for weeks, but waited patiently for me to come around.

That night I called Eric, Debra, and Janet to tell them it was going to happen, and they had a job if they wanted one. All four of us were filled with a large dose of excitement . . . and fear.

I knew we were attempting an impossible task. The only way it would work was if God's hand was on it. But, history told me, that's the way God likes it. When faced with an impossible task like this, life becomes *real and raw.* Our eyes become wide open. We're alert and we make every moment count. And we have no choice but to rely on God.

Here Goes Nothing!

Christmas is an important selling season in the hobby business, so I made it my goal to ensure Horizon Hobby was operational by October 1st. We needed those Christmas sales. My plan was to secure financing in July and then have Eric, Debra, and Janet start August 1st.

We would use August and September to tell hobby shops they could buy from us starting in October, convince manufacturers to sell to us, find a warehouse, lease a computer, select and customize a software system to process orders and run the business, order the right products in the right quantities, buy and set up shelving, receive and stock shipments, hire people for all departments, and pre-sell whatever we could before October 1st. *Phew. Why did I want to do this again?*

Greg Lykins, who had been a close friend of mine for fifteen years, was the President of Busey Bank at the time and a highly respected leader in the community. As I contemplated my next move, Greg was encouraging and suggested if I started Horizon, maybe Busey could be our bank. Not only that, but he was a part of a new venture capital firm (KLM), and they might be able to provide the equity! Greg and I had grown up together in our careers and I thought, *Wouldn't it be cool if it worked out this way? Maybe God laid all this out for me in advance.* Right after the Fourth of July I told Greg I'd decided to move forward and he was as positive as ever. "Just let us know how much will be needed and let's pursue it," he said. I was walking on air.

I completed the business plan, answering every question a good investor would ask: *What's the need I'm trying to fill? How will I fill it? Whom am I filling it for? Why isn't it being filled by others? Why am I the one to do it? What obstacles will I face? What's the competitive landscape? What are the projections? Why are the assumptions made in the budget reasonable?*

I'd been thinking about this for a while, so it was easy to write. It included low, medium, and high goals with corresponding expenses. Projections showed we could make it if we sold just two million dollars the first year; at four million we'd be off and running; and at six million we would be a huge success. To get started I would need a $500,000 credit line to buy all I needed for the infrastructure and inventory. For the bank to provide the credit line I would need $150,000 in equity.

During the second week of July, I completed the business plan and presented it to Greg, hoping for a quick response. In the meantime, I began preliminary work on the startup. Jeanene and I cleared out the basement playroom in our home and bought four used desks to get ready for August 1st. I began searching for computers, software, and warehouse options. And I had a meeting with Clint.

Business Is Business

It was important to talk with Clint before he found out from someone else. I had left him with the impression I would probably take the Herr's position, so I knew he was going to feel blindsided. On Monday, July 8th, I went to his office, sat down across from him, and said, "After a lot of prayer and thought, I've decided to start a hobby distribution company like GP." He was surprised. After an initial pause, he launched into all the reasons why I was making the wrong decision, saying, "You don't have the necessary capital! No chance for success! You will be risking your family's future. You should take the job at Herr's."

I stood my ground and, as our conversation ended, he finished with, "You know, I have a lot of influence in this community and Hobbico has influence in the industry. I like you, Rick, but business is business. You need to understand, I'll do everything possible to protect my investment. That's just the way it is."

I walked to my car with my knees shaking. Who was I kidding? Did I think Clint would just be happy for me and leave me alone? This was shaping up to end in epic failure before I even got started. The only thing that kept me going was to think how this might be God's Promised Land, and I felt Him comfort me. *If Horizon is the right way, God will overcome all the power in the world to bring it to pass.* So I moved forward.

Two weeks later, Greg got back to me, on a Friday. He was very apologetic as he said, "I thought it would be okay and really wanted to do this, but we just can't get involved. Clint is a big customer of

Busey and we can't risk losing his business. We'd love to help but . . . business is business. We have a responsibility to our stockholders."

I felt like I'd been punched in the gut. It took my breath away, but I tried not to show it. I mean, I understood. Clint had a company to protect. The bank had shareholders to answer to. Why hadn't I figured this out before? I guess I just didn't want to think about how hard this was going to be. I preferred to think God had it all laid out for me ahead of time and it would be easy.

Family Matters

In fact, God did have a plan laid out and it was a better one, but it was going to be anything but easy. After my conversation with Greg, I entered the worst weekend I've ever experienced in my life. I was depressed and cried out to God, "Why have You brought me this far just for me to fail?" All weekend, I was in a state of shock. I was angry at myself, embarrassed for being so naïve, and consumed with self-pity. What would people think when I had to give the idea up so quickly? I was like a deer in the headlights, not knowing which way to turn. I felt lost.

In between the awful scenarios playing out in my head and the anger, grief, and stress I felt, God continued to remind me about our Promised Land. Failing before we made even one sale just wasn't consistent with what we thought we'd heard from God. If we understood Him correctly, He would overcome this. And look at Abram! He didn't just fly into Canaan on a private jet and watch all the people who lived there flee. Of course not. It was after four hundred and fifty years and many battles that God's promise was finally fulfilled. This wasn't going to be easy for us, either.

After spending the weekend depressed and miserable, I did the only thing I could do on Monday morning. I hit the pavement. It was now a super tight time frame, so I called banks and investment groups early Monday asking if we could meet "today." I met with six banks and multiple equity prospects that week, presenting the business plan and the "ask" each time. By the end of the week, two banks had given me a commitment letter for a $500,000 credit line if (and only if) I secured $150,000 in equity. I am forever grateful to Gary Wackerlin, Jim Welch, and John Corley for having that kind of confidence in me.

I still needed the equity capital to make it work. Many of the prospects I'd talked with were interested and considering it by the end of July, but no one was on board. Somehow Jeanene and I had enough confidence in God's promise that this didn't slow us down. We went headlong into August and the start of Horizon without the money committed.

On August 1st, Eric, Debra, and Janet started to work in our makeshift basement office. Eric got on the phone with manufacturers and put together orders for those who would sell to us. Many wouldn't, because they were afraid of Hobbico's backlash. Janet and Debra called the hobby shop owners to prepare them for October 1st. In the end, enough agreed to work with us that we were able to keep moving forward.

We needed to finalize artwork for our logo quickly, so we could place ads and prepare marketing materials. One day in early August, Eric leaned over to me (our desks were all squished together in what was once the playroom) and showed me an orange HORIZON with big block letters to signify a strong foundation. I liked it immediately, because God was our foundation—there could be nothing stronger. I said, "I like it; let's use it," and that was that.

While Eric, Janet, and Debra were setting up suppliers and customers, I was busy setting up the framework to process orders and pay the bills. A terrific systems analyst I knew was willing to take a chance with me, so I worked with him to select and customize a software package. We leased an IBM System 36 computer, which was a real workhorse back then. I found an old bowling alley in a small town ten miles north of Champaign-Urbana. It had suffered a fire years earlier and was still in need of repair, but it was 10,000 square feet (the right size) and affordable, assuming we would get financing.

We were making good progress toward opening October 1st, but were now committed for hundreds of thousands of dollars with no way yet to pay for it. I needed to find $150,000—and find it quick! Since that awful weekend in July, I'd presented to over thirty potential investors, but no one would put money in without significant voting control. I was determined to retain at least fifty-one percent control so I could set my own vision and lead Horizon the way I wanted.

My brother and father had said from the beginning they would help, but that was a last resort. If I went down, I didn't want to take them with me. My dad's only significant asset was his retirement account of $50,000 and he was already retired. My brother, Larry, simply didn't have the net worth to make it fly, in my opinion. If Horizon failed, Dad would be left without money for retirement, and Larry would be paying off debt for the rest of his life, while I filed for bankruptcy. Not a pretty picture.

But, as the end of August rolled around, I was out of time. I needed the equity commitment right then in order to borrow on the credit line to pay salaries and the many other bills coming due. I had to take another look at accepting money from my family or give up, shut Horizon down, and file for bankruptcy. So, I considered it.

Maybe, just maybe, I could borrow $75,000 using my name as collateral, Dad could take $37,500 from his retirement, and Larry could borrow $37,500 dollars on his name. That would give us the $150,000 we needed. Jeanene and I talked about it and decided to let my family know where we stood. We would gauge their reaction and go from there. Unless they made it perfectly clear they wanted to invest, we'd close up shop and suffer the consequences.

The very next Sunday, we drove the twenty miles to Monticello, as we often did, for Sunday lunch. When we arrived, my dad and Larry were replacing some shingles on the roof. Jeanene took our three young girls inside to see their grandmother.

"So, where do you stand with financing?" Larry asked in a light-hearted tone, never looking up from his work. They continued working as I quietly said, "I'm out of options. I couldn't get the equity, so it's not going to work."

Immediately, Larry and Dad both responded nonchalantly, "Let us help, then. We always thought this was the right way to go, anyway. Maybe now you'll let us finally help you."

They acted like it was no big deal! They carried on like this is just what family does. I told them my plan of $37,500 from each of them and they said, "Let's do it. Don't worry about it; we'll be fine."

This was the most humbling moment of my life. To think they loved and trusted me that much! Then I thought of God's love and trust in me. My heart was incredibly filled by the love just demonstrated by my heavenly Father, my earthly father, and my brother. That was a once-in-a-lifetime experience.

I didn't jump for joy, or yell, or even get excited. It was a sobering moment because of the immense responsibility I felt. However, the moment also confirmed to Jeanene and me that Horizon was a Promised Land given to us by God. *Horizon was bigger than us.* It was God's company and He was in charge of every detail. He was trusting me to lead it.

I thanked my dad and Larry, whispered a "thank you" to God, and we all went inside for Sunday lunch.

5

Miracles

"Part of happiness is having a Higher Purpose. Something to strive for that is bigger than you. We all want to matter and to make a difference in the world, at work or in someone else's life. Our Higher Purpose is how we find deep meaning and fulfillment in our lives by contributing to someone or something that is bigger than ourselves. Many persons have a wrong idea of what constitutes true happiness. It is not attained through self-gratification but through fidelity to a worthy purpose." —Helen Keller

Throughout August and September, we often worked eighteen-hour days at Horizon in order to meet the promises we had made to be shipping orders by October 1st. In hindsight, we really had no idea how difficult it would be.

Eric was ordering product and placing ads. Janet and Debra were setting up customers and taking pre-orders to get cash rolling as soon as possible (we had a lot to pay back!). I turned the old bowling alley into a distribution facility, hired the people we would soon need, and set up the infrastructure. We ran from one task to another with an unbelievable bias for action.

We didn't see our families much that fall. Jeanene sometimes brought our three girls to Thomasboro (the little town where Horizon started) to play in the warehouse, or to share a picnic dinner in a park nearby, under the water tower with a big smiley face painted on it. Our daughters—Jill, Carrie, and Marnie—were ten, eight, and five, respectively. They loved running around the warehouse, talking with all of our new employees, and pushing each other on the pallet jack. I'm sure OSHA would not have approved, but the girls had a lot of fun.

On Friday afternoons, we would fire up the grill behind the warehouse and have a company picnic. My dad always did the cooking while the rest of us worked. Mom played with the girls and told Dad what to do. They invested a lot of themselves into the company—they were often around Horizon: cleaning, cutting the grass, or doing whatever else needed to be done.

At the Friday picnics we all had fun re-hashing what had happened that week, like who had done something extraordinary or funny, and sharing feedback from customers or vendors. Everyone was equal. What a forklift driver or stocker did that week was just as important as anything I or anyone else did. Our team was one body—one person a foot, another an arm, another a pinkie finger, but any one part was just as important to making the body work as another.

The development of this positive company culture affected us all spiritually as well as mentally and physically. We knew we were a part of something special. And, it was something we wanted to maintain as we grew larger. To that end, we put into words the core of what we were doing and why we were doing it. This formed Horizon's vision, mission, and values, and we talked about it all the time to remind ourselves of what we were striving for—as a company and as a people.

Technical Difficulties

By the end of September, we were almost there but . . . hit a wall. There were orders ready to process October 1st, but we couldn't get the software to work. We struggled with it all night September 30th and into the next morning. Finally, at five a.m., I announced, "Guys, it's time to call it. We did all we could, but we're just not going to be able to open today. Let's go get some rest and we'll try again tomorrow."

For us, it was a colossal failure. We had promised everyone in the industry we'd be shipping orders by October 1st. No one believed us, which is exactly why it was so important to do it. We wanted to show people from the get-go that Horizon was going to be different, that we could be trusted, because we always did what we said we were going to do.

I was ready to give up, but Janet and Debra didn't buy it. "We're not going home," they told me indignantly. "We will get this thing working somehow, and WE WILL ship orders today." And that we did. By late morning Debra had found a way to get around the system so we could print packing slips, and we all headed to the warehouse to pack orders. True to our word, we shipped $72,000 worth of pre-orders on October 1st. Horizon was off and running!

What had been accomplished since July 4th was nothing short of a miracle. Seriously, I'm just not smart enough to pull something like that off on my own! None of us were. Better people than us could have done a lot of things right and still not put this together in less than three months. It was confirmation that we were on the right track. I thanked God for opening doors and aligning the details.

Fulfilling that first promise got the industry's attention. Suddenly, we had the owners of hobby shops and manufacturers cheering for us, the underdogs. It looked like we might even have a chance! Orders kept coming and we shipped every single one the same day it came in. If it meant working late or bringing everyone from the office to the warehouse to pack orders, we did it. We gave the warehouse people little thank-you cards they could sign and stick in each order.

I wrote a personal note on every invoice mailed for several months, just to let customers know how much we appreciated them. We were all tired, but the adrenaline kept pumping. It was exciting, fun, and incredibly rewarding.

Exponential Growth

Horizon's sales grew more quickly than expected. We had not counted on the sudden popularity of radio control (RC) cars. Our business plan was based mostly on sales of RC airplanes and helicopters, but a boom in the car market catapulted us forward. I wondered what part God might have played in that.

By the end of December, in three months' time, we had almost reached our "low" goal for the entire first year: two million dollars. Clearly, Horizon had potential. It was a terrific start, but only the start. March had always been a big month at GP, so I challenged the team with the goal of selling "one million in March." I wanted to celebrate our successes, but I also wanted to keep our people engaged and thinking big.

We met that goal of one million in March and didn't look back. Hobbico kept their word by doing what they could to stop us, but dealers and vendors alike needed an alternative and we were their best bet. Hobbico also had its hands full, consolidating GP and Tower at the same time RC cars were selling like hotcakes. By the end of the first twelve months in business, Horizon's revenues reached a little more than our high goal of six million dollars—which, by the way, cost me a mink coat! Let me explain . . .

During the first few months of building Horizon we were a bit harried, and experienced setback after setback with a few victories laced in between. As someone who has frequently suffered from depression, I let myself live in those setbacks. I wallowed in them.

I tried to show a positive attitude at work in order to encourage and motivate my team, but at home I was a complete mess.

One morning, I was bringing Jeanene up to date on just *how bad things were.* I felt she didn't show enough sympathy for my awful plight, so I said, "It was a good try, Jeanene, but it's just not going to work. I don't see any way out of this one." I was convinced the latest problems would finally be our doom.

However, my self-pity and plea for sympathy had the opposite effect. Jeanene had had enough of my whining! Pointing her finger directly at me, she got right in my face and yelled, "Yes, you are going to start this company and it's going to work! In fact, you're going to reach your high goal in the very first year. And when that happens, you're going to buy me a mink coat! Do you hear me?" Then, she turned around and went back to what she was doing. I was speechless.

As you might imagine, Jeanene didn't forget that little confrontation. When we hit six million dollars in year one, we went shopping.

California Dreamin'

The first five years of Horizon were a whirlwind. Sales doubled almost every year and, although that was great for business, it created one fire after another. We raced to keep inventory in stock and orders shipped on the same day they were received. New people were hired and trained quickly. Bad debts hit us hard when every dollar counted so dearly. Returns cost us money we didn't have. Eventually, the warehouse filled up and we needed to find a bigger one, followed by moving the entire company in a long weekend. We couldn't afford even a single day without sales. When power, phones, or the mainframe went down, it was a complete crisis.

Cash was a scarce commodity. Every few months, I had to return to our bank asking for a larger credit line. The lack of cash flow was always my greatest stressor. I hated running out of money and being broke when it was time to pay bills. Yet, it was important to take advantage of the opportunities before us, so we kept pushing the envelope. For us, this meant expansion.

I knew we needed a warehouse on the West Coast. It just took too long to deliver goods from Illinois, over the Rockies, and all the way to the West. Small hobby shops relied on our fast delivery to keep their consumers happy. Making our customers wait more than a week for shipments to arrive was simply not acceptable.

In the spring of '86, I felt like it was the right time to open a sales and distribution center in California. It would differentiate us from Hobbico and show the industry we were in this for the long haul. I flew into LAX by myself with no contacts, no meetings—just a mission and a whole lot of passion. The only thing I knew to do was visit the Chamber of Commerce upon arriving in each city to make connections and generate leads.

Oxnard and Ventura were my first stops, but no one gave me the time of day. Horizon was too small and too new for them to even bother. The rejections mounted as I went up the coast. Unfazed, I kept going north, stopping in city after city until I got to the middle of the state. When I arrived in San Luis Obispo, I remembered that Jeanene and I had visited there during a 1974 camping vacation. We had loved it because it was fresh, natural, on the ocean, and a college town, like our home in Illinois. *Maybe this is where God has been leading me from the start!* Unfortunately, that thought was quickly extinguished when I met with the Chamber. It was a Central Coast community dominated by leftover hippies and Cal Poly students. I still loved it, but business was not welcome there.

I was running out of options. Defeated. Tired. Weary. Going further north would likely get more expensive and less business friendly. I began to wonder if I'd misread God. *Had I just been hearing what I wanted to hear?* Just as I was ready to give up and book a ticket home, a local real estate agent showed a little interest. A glimmer of hope! He said there was a building for lease at a small airport in Paso Robles, thirty miles north of San Luis Obispo. It was a 10,000-square-foot building on Propeller Drive and the price was right. It was off the beaten path, making shipping more difficult, but otherwise, it was perfect for an RC airplane and car distribution center. We leased the entire building.

I believed this was another example of God showing up, after I'd done everything I could do, proving that He's always with me and will bring forth His plans when I'm ready to listen. It's often when I get to the end of my rope that something really good happens.

Another miracle was waiting for me upon my return to Champaign. As soon as I told my brother Larry that Horizon was opening a West Coast Distribution Center, he said, "How about me moving there to run Horizon West for you?" I tried to talk him out of it because he already had a lot at risk. If he did this and Horizon failed, he would not only be deep in debt, but he wouldn't have a job! This was a crazy idea. It was not only too risky for him, but he was a loan officer at a bank—he had no experience leading an organization.

On paper it made no sense, but Larry felt in his heart it was the right thing to do and I knew there was no one I could trust more to run Horizon West. We both had peace about the decision, as did our wives. So, just like that, it was done. This was the beginning of a powerful partnership between two brothers with very different skills and personalities. Larry was a gift from God to Jeanene and me—one we had nothing to do with, other than having the wisdom to accept the gift.

The early years of Horizon Hobby were amazing. So many miracles, one after the other, fell into place. The three people I needed to start Horizon were available at just the right time, and others with our values and a strong work ethic were there to join us. Enough dealers took a risk and placed orders with us, and a uniquely qualified consultant was available to get us into the right computing system. My Dad, brother, and father-in-law (who wanted to invest ten thousand dollars when he learned Dad and Larry were investing) were the only shareholders who would have allowed me to reinvest all profits so we could keep growing, and the right bankers took a risk with us while the wrong ones shied away. A warehouse in Thomasboro just happened to be available, I found a warehouse on the West Coast (on Propeller Drive), and my brother stepped up to the plate to run it . . . and so on. The miracles never ceased.

A Higher Purpose

Jeanene and I started Horizon because we believed a business could be the most fun, meaningful, efficient, and profitable when it is run with God's principles at the center. We were convinced an environment based on biblical values was not only better for people, it was a recipe for a better business. So far, that was proving to be true. It certainly felt like God was involved every step of the way.

Many companies have a higher purpose that makes them more fulfilling for everyone involved. For example, *Mary Kay Cosmetics*—to enrich women's lives; *Patagonia*—to build the best product, cause no unnecessary harm, and to use business to inspire implementation of solutions to the environmental crisis; *Chick-fil-a*—to glorify God and to have a positive influence on all who come into contact with the business; and *Apple*—to create innovations in computer technology that change the world.

These are all big visions that inspire me; they fire me up and make me want to jump on board! If I worked for any of those companies, I'd go above and beyond the call of duty to help achieve their purpose.

We wanted to create a special business with a higher purpose. We figured that people spend more hours of their day at work than anywhere else. What if work was a place that inspired people to love each other and treat everyone like we would like to be treated? All kinds of good things would come from that. Strong, caring relationships would be built with customers, manufacturers, suppliers, and everyone our people came into contact with. Service levels would be excellent. And, the same attitude would bleed over into employees' personal lives, making them better spouses, parents, friends, and citizens.

Over time we refined our Vision, Mission, and Values so everyone at Horizon would understand what we were striving for. We knew we wouldn't be perfect at it, but it was the essence of who we were. We put it on a wallet card and explained it carefully to every employee at orientation. The "20 Basics" were designed to describe what the values look like in practice. We reinforced them in regular department huddles and at quarterly meetings, and every morning a "Basic" would pop up on their computer screen. I handed the wallet card to visitors freely, impressing upon them, "This is all you need to know about Horizon."

Displayed on our wallet card were the vision, mission, and values that shaped the culture of Horizon Hobby:

Our Vision

To see the world
impacted by God
through the influence of
Horizon and its people.

Our Mission

We help people have fun
with hobbies.

Our Values

Golden Rule

Treat each other, each customer, and each supplier with utmost respect as we would best like to be treated ourselves.

Customer Is Boss

A caring, "can-do" attitude in every situation.

Inverted Pyramid

A servant leadership model[2]
that leads by *making others better.*

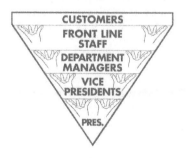

---

2. Greenleaf, Robert K. *The Servant as Leader.* Westfield, IN: Greenleaf Center for Servant Leadership, 2008.

Horizon Basics

1. Each customer will be treated as we would like to be treated if we were the customer.
2. We will put our employees first, because if they are satisfied, dedicated, and energetic, they will treat our customers with warmth, friendliness, and fun.
3. The end user is the ultimate customer we must satisfy. We will sell to and service consumers through whatever channel they find most convenient.
4. We will bring high quality, innovative products to market that will ensure a successful hobby experience. Excellent value is more important than offering the lowest price.
5. Consumers are most likely to enjoy their hobby experience when a local hobby shop supports them, so we will develop systems and processes to aid the dealer in serving consumers more successfully and profitably.
6. Dealers and consumers will be provided with the most useful product and industry information in the most easily accessible manner.
7. Each employee will listen to dealers and consumers and deliver solutions that anticipate and satisfy their needs.
8. Customers will not have to wait to place orders or receive answers to their questions.
9. Our shipping will be neat and accurate and same day for all orders received before noon, or even later than noon whenever possible.
10. Fill rates will be extraordinarily high with a goal of 90 percent or better.
11. Working safely will always be more important than the job being done.

12. Any employee who receives a customer complaint "owns" the complaint and is empowered to resolve it and prevent a repeat occurrence.

13. Each employee will continuously identify defects throughout our company.

14. Protecting the assets of Horizon is the responsibility of every employee.

15. Each employee will understand their work responsibilities and welcome being held accountable by all other team members to perform those responsibilities at the highest level.

16. Smile. We are on stage and smiles transcend even phone lines. Use proper vocabulary with our customers. Use words or phrases like, "Certainly. I'll be happy to. It's my pleasure."

17. Be an ambassador of Horizon inside and outside the workplace. Always speak positively. You are part of Horizon so remember that every comment reflects on you too. Take pride in Horizon and show it.

18. Use the customer's name often (external customers and employees) to express importance, respect, and warmth.

19. Be yourself. Reflect your own personality in a genuine manner—relaxed and comfortable, yet always professional.

20. Have fun. Enjoy your job. A good attitude is infectious.

The Vision describes WHY we did what we did; the Mission describes WHAT we did, and the Values describe HOW we did it. This was our Higher Purpose and we knew it would only be achieved by God's grace and involvement. We were amazed, but not surprised, with how the purpose of Horizon became reality and so many people were blessed because of it.

What happened was nothing short of a miracle.

6

When Disaster Strikes

*"Aslan is a lion, **the** Lion, the great Lion."*
"Oh," said Susan. "I'd thought he was a man. Is he quite safe?
I shall feel rather nervous about meeting a lion . . ."
"Safe?" said Mr. Beaver. "Who said anything about safe? Of
course he isn't safe. But he's good. He's the King, I tell you."[3]

I love this quote from the C.S. Lewis' famous book, *The Lion, the Witch, and the Wardrobe.* Here, Lewis is using allegory to tell the reader a deeper truth that, like Aslan—the lion king of Narnia—God is good, but He isn't safe. It's "dangerous" to be around Him because He leads us into risks we would never take ourselves. But oh, what an adventure it is to follow Him and experience the joy of doing more than we ever thought we could!

Risk. Excitement. Adventure. Thrill. Uncertainty. Life is not easy by any means, because doing anything great is not easy. But God knows us and loves us, and everything He leads us into is good, whether it looks that way or not. I truly believe that following God

---

3. In the first book in the *Chronicles of Narnia* series, *The Lion, The Witch, and The Wardrobe*, by C.S. Lewis, we read of this conversation between Mr. Beaver and Susan.

is the only way to experience an abundant life. Living only to please ourselves can't begin to compare.

This is the message that was gradually piercing my heart as my career unfolded. My life on Earth was tangible and real, but one drastically limited compared to living it with God. Life became more robust and profound when my physical experiences were framed within the context of God's love and His plan for me.

In just five years, Horizon had gone from nothing more than an idea to fifty million dollars in revenue with a profit every month of our existence. My physical life was looking pretty exciting and successful, but my spiritual life was even better. Inside, I felt the magnificence of God as I followed Him on this risky journey. His plan for me was turning out to be much grander than anything I could've dreamed up. But still, He wasn't done with me.

A Need for More

In April 1990, something unexpected happened. Inexplicably, the bottom dropped out of the R/C car market. The sudden boom in the car market had gotten us off to a fast start. Now, it ended just as quickly as it had begun. We went from doubling sales every year to zero growth, seemingly overnight. That was a serious problem!

When a company is growing quickly, it's hard to hire people and increase your infrastructure as quickly as necessary. As a result, profits tend to be higher during periods of fast growth. On the other hand, it's hard to stop the momentum of increasing personnel and infrastructure costs when growth dries up. To make it worse, profit margins get squeezed when sales slow, as companies lower prices to maintain volume and stay in business.

As a third-party distributor of the exact same products our competitors sold, margins were low to begin with. When the car market nosedived, competitive pricing took hold and we saw our margins sink to under 10 percent. It was simply unsustainable. All of us at Horizon were terrified.

It became crystal clear that we needed a different business model—one better suited to long-term viability. We couldn't survive as a "middleman." The most fitting method to improve profit margins was to develop product lines no one else had—exclusive lines only Horizon sold. If they were innovative and high quality, we could charge more than competitors charged for similar items because customers would want the better products (along with our excellent service, of course.) The question was how to get there without investing millions of dollars over a period of years for "research and development." We didn't have the capital nor the time.

The fastest method was to become the exclusive distributor of high-quality product lines presently sold through multiple distributors, none of which were committed to selling their products over their competitors'. It was a big step for any significant manufacturer to entrust its line with a company that had only been in existence a few years. But, I had to try. There was one manufacturer in particular that would change the trajectory of Horizon instantly . . . so I hopped on a plane to Tokyo.

I went to Japan with my accountant and good friend, Mike Martin, to convince this large company and our anchor brand—Futaba radios—to put all of their trust in us. We were ushered into a conference room filled with executives—I counted thirty-two of them! Mr. Hosoya, the president of the entire organization (of which R/C was just one division) was "the man." He was trim, healthy, and the only one in the room as tall as my friend and me. He had a friendly smile and clearly was revered by his managers and other executives.

Mr. Hosoya gave me the floor. For about three hours. I explained in great detail the R/C industry landscape in the US, why Futaba needed a single distributor with a deep-seated incentive to market their products over all others, how Horizon filled that need like no other, and what the future for them looked like with and without Horizon as their exclusive distributor. In the end, I offered them the opportunity to buy a share of Horizon in return for making Horizon their exclusive distributor.

Mr. Hosoya and the other representatives listened intently and knew it all made sense. I could see it in their eyes. When I finished answering all their questions, a multitude of side conversations in Japanese erupted. It was almost comical as we sat and listened. We couldn't understand a single word—and the many conversations were LOUD! Finally, Mr. Hosoya took the floor.

He sat directly across from me and looked me square in the eyes. He said he agreed with my synopsis of the US market and felt Horizon would be a good partner. However, he said, "Futaba will stick with multiple distributors in the US rather than a single exclusive distributor for its products. That's how it's done in Japan and it should be done the same way in the US." Then he added, "But if I ever want to sell my company, I want you to make the presentation for me." Everything worked as well as I could have hoped except for one small detail: the answer was no.

When My Own Plans Are Not Enough

When I went to Japan to make this offer, I was doing what I thought needed to be done for Horizon. On paper, the partnership looked like a deal made in Heaven. But, in retrospect, I was acting out of fear rather than faith in God's plan for us. What started as a beautiful blessing from God—Horizon Hobby—had turned sour, and I didn't have the capital to survive this market downturn. Profits had disappeared and I was ready to run for safety. I wanted God to bail me out, because the future without Futaba as a Horizon exclusive line looked impossible. I didn't know what else to do.

I realize now (hindsight is always 20/20) that selling Futaba a share of Horizon would've been a great deal for them and a horrible deal for Horizon. Sure, it would have helped Horizon in the short run, but even if Futaba were a minority owner, it would have totally derailed our very reason for starting the company. We would have lost control of our vision, because whoever controls the purse strings controls the company. I had taken my eyes off God and was running to where I thought I'd be safer.

The need to change our business model remained, but I realized I needed to do it without losing control of the company. I tried to negotiate an exclusive arrangement with a number of other manufacturers after Futaba fell through, but to no avail. Nothing seemed to work and I became impatient with God.

Margins continued to slide, losses mounted, and credit became tight. We cut expenses everywhere we could until there was nothing left to cut. As things got worse, my depression and anxiety increased, which had a negative effect on my decision-making and home life. It was difficult to think clearly when my mind was filled with worry.

When it was time for our strategic planning retreat in 1991, we had exhausted most every option to acquire notable exclusive brands and our failure was showing in the numbers. Our managers and I were becoming more fearful about our prospects for the future. I had hoped to come out of the retreat with new ideas and renewed energy, leading to a new business model. However, the consensus of the team was that we couldn't afford to take any big risks—we needed to just do what we were doing, but do it better. Our objectives for the next two years revolved around growing revenues organically through improvements in service. It was very uninspiring and a most disappointing retreat.

I consider this era to be my leadership at its worst. Organizations don't succeed when decisions are made by consensus. This has been proven time and again in history, and in the stories we read in the Bible about God's dealings with the nation of Israel. When there is a lack of strong leadership the void always gets filled, and it usually gets filled with the loudest voices who are the last ones to provide good leadership.

Reflection and Change

Reflecting afterwards on the retreat, I hastened back to the biblical example of the Israelites attempting to enter the Promised Land. Moses miraculously led God's people out of bondage in Egypt to the edge of the Promised Land. But, when the advance team of twelve returned from spying out the land (Canaan), only Joshua and Caleb said, "We should go up and take possession of the land, for we can certainly do it." The other ten said "We can't attack those people; they are stronger than we are." *It's risky, scary, and the people are too strong. It's not safe. We can't do this! We were better off in Egypt.* When the going got tough and people complained, Moses listened to the majority—and they spent the next forty years in the desert as a result (Numbers 13:17-14:10).

Like Moses, I had a weak moment and listened to the majority at our '91 retreat. Not surprisingly, the outcome was a dead end. This was a time when Horizon needed a strong leader who stayed on target and brought everyone along with him. Instead, I failed. It didn't seem like God was answering my prayers, so I gave in. Yet, I continued to pray that if I was on the wrong track, God would show me. Finally, something happened. I didn't know if it was good or bad, but it was something.

Over the years, I had talked periodically with Bill Bennett, who was an avid R/C modeler and owner of Circus Circus, Luxor, and several other Las Vegas casinos. As an extension of his hobby, he also owned Hobby Dynamics (a distributor, like Horizon and GP) and Circus Hobbies (a direct mail company like Tower). However, these two companies had never performed well and the recession in our industry had made it worse. Losses were piling up for Mr. Bennett and he was looking for a solution.

In early 1992, he contacted me to discuss buying Horizon and merging it with his own company. His pitch was that merging the two companies would solve a lot of problems for me. He figured the low margins had to be hurting us badly and this would give me a way out. His capital, his exclusive lines, and my leadership would put us in excellent position to compete with Hobbico.

It made a lot of sense, but I knew I would not be happy going back to leading a company I didn't own. It was tempting, though, because I was worried and simply had no other good ideas. Or did I? Suddenly, a wild thought came to mind. What if we bought *his company* instead of Bennett buying ours? It would give us the high-quality, under-marketed exclusive brands we had been searching for, eliminate a low-price competitor (Hobby Dynamics), and I would still own the company. We didn't have the money to do it, but Bennett was rich—maybe he would finance the purchase. So, I said to Mr. Bennett, "Let's meet."

Not One Dollar Higher

The next day, Eric Meyers and I headed to Las Vegas to make our proposal. Bill seemed interested. We presented a strong case and it worked. In that meeting we reached a deal—we would buy Hobby Dynamics and Circus Hobbies for fair market value of their inventory and fixed assets. The exclusive agreements he had with overseas manufacturers were not transferable, but he would help us try to secure them. We would give him one million dollars at closing and pay the rest over the next two years.

It was a huge risk for us—a "bet-the-farm" kind of risk. Either this would transform us into a leader in the industry, or send us into bankruptcy. We would have to borrow another million and didn't know how we'd pay the rest to Bill in just two years. It would put us in competition with some of our loyal manufacturers, including Futaba, and they would not be happy. And we had no assurance that Bennett's manufacturers would accept an almost bankrupt Horizon as their exclusive agent in place of a wealthy Bill Bennett. However, if it worked, it would change Horizon from a third-party distributor living on borrowed time to an exclusive distributor of our own strong brands.

I spent a lot of time praying about this deal. The lack of profit had taken its toll. We were vulnerable. I prayed, "Lord God, give me a sign! If buying these companies is the right thing to do for Your company, make it clear. And if it's wrong, make it just as clear. May Your will be done, Lord, not my own."

Every morning I prayed, entrusting it to God. Finally, we came to a roadblock when it came to valuing their inventory. They showed a total cost of nine million dollars, which is what Bill wanted to be paid for it. However, we knew that much of their inventory was old and would have to be sold below cost or even thrown away. Finally, we set up a conference call to try to reach an agreement. This call was the "make it or break it" call that would determine our future.

While praying that morning, a word from God came to me that was crystal clear: seven million dollars was the right value for the inventory. If Bill came down to this number, God's answer regarding the purchase was a resounding "yes." If it was even one dollar higher than seven million, I would let Hobby Dynamics and Circus Hobbies go.

Our product team had prepared details about every single item that was questionable. I knew little about what would or wouldn't sell, but had complete trust in Eric and his team. We got our ducks in a row and then called Bill. He had two or three modelers on his end to argue their case.

We spent hours on that call, because I just wasn't going to budge. If it weren't for my prayer that morning, and the whisper I'd received from God, I probably would have folded early, just to get the deal done. Bill finally came down to $7.1M and thought for sure that would do it. It didn't. Not one dollar higher than seven million or I'd let it go. In the end, Bill accepted seven million and that was my answer. I believed it was proof once again that when I let God into what I'm doing, He is involved in every aspect of it, even in the math of deal-making.

A New Path Forward

We closed on HD/Circus in July of 1992. I was both excited and terrified. My CFO and I went to Las Vegas to sign the contracts. After enjoying a celebratory dinner with Bill, we took the red-eye back to Champaign to meet with all the employees in the morning. We had managed to keep the news of our negotiations quiet, so no one in our company or the industry knew. Meetings at Horizon and HD were scheduled back-to-back that morning, starting as soon as our plane landed.

The response from Horizonites was excitement, along with a huge dose of concern as to whether we could pull this off. Hobby Dynamics employees were subdued and fearful of losing their jobs as we combined the two companies. I tried to allay their fears, but none of us really knew what was to come. I was positive, but also honest with them.

Then we went to work communicating to the industry our plans for this new company. We had scripts for our people to use, press releases, and lists of industry people to call personally ready to go. We wanted to make the announcement to everyone at the same time and with a consistent message.

Finding our way through the maze of merging Horizon and Hobby Dynamics (we closed Circus Hobbies) successfully would turn out to be far more difficult than we had imagined. It's a good thing I didn't know what lay ahead or I never would have pulled the trigger. I think that's the way God works, though. He knows that if in the beginning I had seen the deep valley to come, I would have taken another route—a safer route—like Moses when he turned back from going into the Promised Land.

7

Hitting Rock Bottom

When God points me in a certain direction, and it's obvious the directive is from Him, I think, *Great! Things have finally turned around, and now that I know God's plan, everything will be better.* Of course, His perspective is so much different than mine. And, He usually has a much better plan than I could ever imagine for myself.

I felt this way after acquiring HD. Horizon would finally have the exclusive product lines we needed and eliminate a low-price competitor in the process. I believed God had answered my prayers and Horizon would now be able to remake itself with a new business model and start growing again. I thought, *Isn't God good? For several years I've tried to find the exclusive products needed to move forward but only found closed doors. And just when I was about ready to give up, HD comes along.* I was convinced we simply needed to be good stewards and success would finally return.

But, two major unforeseen setbacks changed everything.

Disaster Strikes Again

Before buying HD, I had spent a lot of time with York Daimon and Mr. Yamamoto, who ran Futaba USA. Futaba was our anchor line, responsible for about nine of our fifty-million-dollar revenue stream. I couldn't afford to lose Futaba, no way. However, HD's anchor exclusive line—and our most prized possession in the purchase—was JR Radios, a direct competitor to Futaba.

HD sold only about one million dollars' worth of JR and they were the only distributor selling it. Futaba sold about sixty million of their radio line through Hobbico, Horizon, and at least fifteen smaller distributors. Our pitch to Futaba this time was that JR wasn't a viable competitor in this part of the world, it was too expensive for modelers to switch from Futaba to JR even if they wanted to, and since Futaba was such a high percentage of Horizon sales, we couldn't afford NOT to sell their line as hard as ever.

York and Mr. Yamamoto didn't like it, but they liked us and wanted to keep supporting us. They went to bat for us with Mr. Hosoya in Tokyo, but it was hard for them to believe that we wouldn't focus on JR over Futaba. York was noncommittal, but he didn't try to talk me out of buying HD either. In the end, we thought we bought enough from them, and that they wouldn't cut us off. We were wrong.

A few weeks after we closed on HD, I received a one-sentence fax from Futaba in Tokyo stating they would no longer sell their line to Horizon. No further explanation. When I read that little fifteen-word fax, I froze. I couldn't speak, couldn't move; I just stood there, looking at the piece of paper. I'd bought a company with seventeen million in annual sales, and had just lost nine million in Horizon sales because of it!

The second thing that happened cost us the other half of HD's seventeen-million-dollar revenue stream. We'd gone through their customer list during our due diligence process, and knew they were selling to large mail order companies at very low prices to get more volume. We had good relationships with these same customers, because they bought some products from us as well. We believed we could save most of this volume at slightly higher prices since HD was gone and our service was better. After the purchase, we did everything we could to retain their business. Unfortunately, they found other suppliers who would meet their price demands. This cost us about seven million of HD's sales volume.

The net result of these two unforeseen potholes? Within six months of buying HD, almost its entire seventeen-million-dollar revenue stream had vanished. Yet, we had picked up all of its expense base and still owed Mr. Bennett seven million dollars over the next two years! We'd made a colossal miscalculation. Horizon had been barely getting by for the past two years, and now things were even worse. We were in a hole so deep, it looked impossible to ever climb out.

God Loves the Impossible

Have you ever noticed that God loves to show up when a situation seems impossible? It seems to me that's where He often does His best work—in impossible situations. When I was working at a dead-end job and going nowhere a year after my college graduation, when I lost my job at RP, when I lost my job at GP, when I was at the end of my rope because I couldn't get the financing to start Horizon . . . God had stepped in. Every one of those situations looked impossible, but He always made a way.

I knew in my head that times like this had been the most exciting of my life, and this would be no exception. I was *forced* to rely on God alone all those times, which put me in a good place. However, in my heart I didn't believe it. I was angry with God and prayed, "I don't get it! How could You let this happen? I prayed throughout this entire process and felt like You were leading me to buy HD. But look at where we are now! Horizon is in ten times worse shape now and I have no idea where to go from here. How could You do this to me?"

I felt like God's answer to that prayer was simply, "Trust me." That helped for a brief moment, but reality was bashing me in the face at the same time. Yes, God had pulled me through the impossible before, but this one looked different. I slipped back into depression and I fell hard. I felt like a huge failure and, as hard as I tried, I couldn't let it go.

I reverted back to feeling sorry for myself. Jeanene always caught the brunt of my mood disorder because she was the only person to whom I could reveal my weaknesses. As a business owner and the leader of Horizon, I had to keep my head up, be positive, and show confidence to hundreds of people even in the worst of times, regardless of how depressed I was.

This time my depression hit its worst stage. I had felt down and depressed plenty of times before, but it seemed reasonably within the realm of normal. I mean, other people were anxious sometimes, too. Maybe this constant worry was necessary to be a great leader. In the past, this was how I rationalized my mood disorder. But this time, I spiraled downward.

Getting out of a Dark Place

In the late '80s, our family had begun spending most of August each year in Snowmass, Colorado. We loved the mountains, cool mornings, fresh smells, aspen leaves glittering in the wind, and the many activities we could enjoy outside together. But 1992 was different. I spent very little time with the family that August. I was home in Illinois, by myself, stewing about the pickle we were in, trying to find a way out. I prayed, worried, thought about how much better things had been before HD, and played out how I would navigate bankruptcy. It really looked like the decision to buy HD would take Horizon down.

On the morning of my forty-fourth birthday, I was sitting at my desk alone, asking God why this was happening to me, and suddenly realized that my constant worry (in both good times and bad times) could not be normal. God surely didn't intend for me to go through life this way, right? It was so frustrating to think that God offered me an abundant life, but I filled mine with worry instead of peace and joy. Something was seriously wrong, but I didn't know what to do about it.

At that moment a thought came to mind, maybe from the Holy Spirit. "Rick, you've lived forty-four years controlled by circumstances, high as a kite one day and hitting rock bottom the next. You'll probably live to be about eighty-eight years old, so half of your life has been spent thinking about how bad things are or how bad things could be. It's time to stop it!" I did not want to live the next forty-four years of my life depressed. I had to do something different.

What I didn't know until much later was what Jeanene was thinking for two days as she was driving the girls home from Colorado. She was tired of being my dumping ground of catastrophic thoughts. More than twenty years of it had been enough, and on the drive home she was contemplating what to do. It didn't look like I was going to change and she couldn't live the rest of her life under this cloud. As hard as it would be, perhaps the only solution was to part ways.

As soon as they returned, I rushed to tell Jeanene what I'd been thinking, because I knew how difficult my depression had been for her. She is a fun-loving, cup-half-full kind of person and I was draining her of all things good. I explained to her that I was going to live my next forty-four years differently; I didn't know how yet, but I was determined to change.

Later, she told me that this was the only thing that circumvented the discussion she planned on having about leaving me.

Depression is like alcoholism in many ways, so she was far from convinced I'd stick with my plan. But, apparently, it gave her enough hope to give it a try.

I began to look for a way out of the depression. I turned to my close friends, pastors, counselors, even one religious extremist from Wichita, Kansas—anyone with an idea of how to get past this. Of course, there was no silver bullet and it took time, but, finally, something clicked. My friend and counselor, Mike Campion, said something that changed my direction completely.

I had been feeling like my counseling sessions with him were going nowhere. Horizon was getting worse by the moment, I was working harder and harder trying to turn things around, and I just didn't have time for counseling, especially if it wasn't helping me. One day in his office, I told Mike I was done. He tried to talk me out of it. I listened, but was in flight mode, much like I had been years ago with Dave Larsen. I just wanted to get out of there and back to work.

Mike wasn't letting up, so finally, I rose to leave. He kept talking. I put my hand on the door. He kept talking. I was doing my best to get out of there when, suddenly, he stood up and walked around his desk. As I quickly walked out the door he said, *"Rick, you're always ruminating about the past or worrying about the future. You never live in the present."*

That got my attention. I stopped in my tracks, looked back toward Mike, and said something like, "You're probably right, but I have to get back to work," and ran out of his office. What Mike said made a tremendous amount of sense, but I had no idea what to do with it.

Something's Gotta Give

I thought about Mike's statement, prayed about it, and tried my best to grasp it. I wanted to live in the present, but I just couldn't seem to do it. I couldn't stop ruminating about how much better things used to be, or stop worrying constantly about what I was going to do when the sky fell. But, very gradually, I began to realize there was another way.

I remembered that Jesus said, "I have come that they might have life, and that they might have it more abundantly."[4] Also, that the apostle Paul suggested in his letter to the Philippians that we don't have to be anxious all the time; instead, we can have a peace that surpasses all understanding.[5] I was determined to live that way my next forty-four years.

I noticed little change right away. Depression is not an addiction that can be conquered once and for all and put in the past. It's something I will always deal with, like a physical illness without a cure. But, it won't kill me, and I've learned to deal with it in a positive fashion.

The first step in my process toward joy and inner peace was to find a few tricks to redirect my mind when negative thoughts begin to haunt me. These included things like **smile**—because that physical act is incongruous with feeling down in the dumps (we don't smile because we're happy; we're happy because we smile), **reach out to others**—because when you are genuinely caring for other people, your own problems tend to fade away, "**just do it**"—because taking action supersedes the time spent worrying about what action to take, **participate, don't spectate**—because actively engaging with others eliminates comparisons that come to mind from just watching them, and **count my blessings**—because there is more to be thankful for than we think.

---

4. John 10:10
5. Philippians 4:6-7

These tactics helped considerably to get me on the right track, but I still struggled. I believed as a Christian, with God's help, I should be able to do this. However, I came to believe that my ailment was more than just mental—it was physical. Maybe my body just wasn't producing enough serotonin. After about ten years of working on it without meds, I decided to give them a try and the difference they made for me was significant.

I hit my low point in 1992. Since my forty-fourth birthday decision, taking one small step after another, I've gotten better at dealing with depression and anxiety and can truthfully say I'm living an abundant life of joy and peace today, most of the time.

But, as I worked toward a better me, Horizon's health continued to decline. Like all the times before when our backs had been against the wall, the only thing we could do was get busy and find a way to make it work. In spite of the reality of the failure we were in the midst of, I believed God had, in fact, led us to acquire HD. So I still believed it had to have been the right move. The main reason for the purchase remained: we had an anchor exclusive line in JR Radios (hopefully), and it was the leader in quality throughout the rest of the world.

Additionally, HD had provided us with other exclusive product lines of helicopters and engines that gave us a small but scalable base. Our job was to increase demand for these brands, so we would have something to sell that was different from other distributors. Our singular focus became to make Horizon brands the best in the business.

A Better Future

The first order of business was to get a signed agreement with JR Radios. We invited the top executives to visit us in Champaign and get to know us. They came in full force and Mr. Oishi was in the lead. He arrived angry, snarling, and aggressively disrespectful.

Eric, Janet, and I sat across from them in our small conference room. Mr. Ito and Mr. Kuyama began to perspire as Mr. Ooishi lambasted us, obviously believing we were no match for JR Radios. We listened kindly and answered each one of his objections, while making the case that Horizon was the only company that had the ability to help JR achieve its potential in North America.

Our first meetings were tough and direct, but set the stage for a great relationship over the next twenty years. We developed a lot of respect for each other in those initial negotiations. We signed an exclusive agreement and set out to turn JR into the leading radio line in America.

We started by trimming the extra overhead gained from the acquisition to position ourselves to make a profit as soon as possible. Next, we began working with our new exclusive manufacturers to get products that better fit the desires of US consumers—products with features that would set us apart. And we started marketing our exclusive lines like they already were the best in the business.

Slowly, we began to coax consumers to give JR radios another look. Eric developed a campaign that made it economical for users to switch to JR, even though they may have had a large investment in incompatible Futaba equipment. We positioned JR as a little more expensive, but worth it, since the quality and workmanship were better. Soon our strategy began to get traction and, as modelers experienced the quality of JR, sales began to grow. It was a miracle!

About a year after the HD purchase, I received a fax from Mr. Gen Saito, the leading manufacturer of four-cycle engines for RC aircraft in the entire world. He wanted to come visit. He and his right-hand man (who spoke English) were in my office a week later. Mr. Saito seldom traveled, but, in retrospect, I think he wanted to meet me in person to see if he could trust me. We hit it off immediately. He was a very nice man and incredibly loyal. The prestigious Saito line was another boost to our reputation.

I loved working with suppliers from all over the world and developed great relationships with them all. But, I always had a soft spot in my heart for Mr. Saito. He was one of the founders of the worldwide RC hobby market and a man of strong principles. He spoke no English and I don't know of his faith walk, but I always felt I could see God in his eyes. It was such an encouragement to have this highly respected man seek us out.

Throughout the 1990s, Horizon continued to gain market share. Our success marketing JR and Saito attracted other exclusive lines for distribution in the US, and we were beginning to design and develop more exclusive products in-house, using manufacturers in Thailand, Taiwan, China, Japan, Russia, and Europe to build to our specifications. As I look back on it today, I see that God's plan to acquire HD was right (again), though it was certainly not the one I would have taken on my own.

Hindsight

I had tried very hard to hold onto Futaba and those nine million dollars' worth of sales, but losing the line was exactly what needed to happen for our long-term success. JR would never have become the leading radio line in North America if all our promotions had been tempered to keep Futaba happy.

Some will tell you that the history of Horizon Hobby is a great American success story. "Rick was out of a job, saw an opportunity, risked everything he and his family had to start a company in his basement, worked hard, overcame overwhelming odds, and became an international leader in the hobby industry." It was a real Horatio Alger story—rags to riches through hard work, determination, courage, and honesty. But, that's not the real story.

The real story is that God had a plan and every time I trusted Him enough to follow my gut, to follow His Spirit within me, I moved closer to that plan. Whenever I felt like I could figure it out on my own or just didn't have time for God, I wandered around in the wilderness for a while. But, it was all part of the long journey with Him.

8

Leading a Culture, Not Just a Company

I woke up in a sweat. My hands were tingling and my heart was racing—I knew what I had to tell the sales department and had been rehearsing it in my head over and over again. It was finally time to tell sales—and the rest of the world, for that matter—that we had just bought a mail-order company.

Up to this time, one of the easiest selling points for our sales team to use was that we didn't bypass hobby shops to sell directly to consumers, like Hobbico did with Tower. For thirteen years, our mantra had been, "We are the dealer's friend! We don't compete with them for sales." But, now that Horizon would be selling directly to consumers, we were eliminating a key differentiating factor. The sales team was going to kill me.

As frustrating as it would be for them to embrace new selling points, it was 1998 and I knew we needed to keep up with the changing business environment. Horizon's exclusive brands were gaining acceptance, but our marketing reach was hindered by the industry-wide three-step distribution system. We couldn't always depend on hobby shops to promote Horizon brands, because they sold whatever brand was easiest and most profitable for them to sell. If they could have more success selling a brand that competed with ours, they would sell it over our brand, and I didn't blame them. To reach our full potential, we needed to make the sale if the dealer didn't, and that required direct contact with consumers.

At the same time, the internet was gaining momentum and a new company called Amazon was selling books directly to consumers very successfully. Early adopters were beginning to trust the internet and Horizon needed to prepare to be in that arena. Though dealers would remain our primary customer, there would be times when we were going to sell directly to consumers, and we needed to have that flexibility.

With much trepidation, I asked our sales team to gather in the big learning room upstairs. These people were on the frontlines with dealers. If our salespeople didn't believe in the strategy, there was no way the dealers would, and this was going to be a tough sell to Horizonites.

When I started the meeting with, "We just acquired a mail-order company," there was a collective gasp in the room. They were stunned. This sales team loved what Horizon stood for. They had presented Horizon for years as the people dealers could trust, and we always stood behind them to keep our word. Now, they would have to get on the phone and explain to their "friends" we had changed course, and somehow make them believe it was going to be good for them.

Our strategy was a sound one, though, and this is what I needed the sales team to understand. Mail-order companies filled the magazines with advertising for the same products dealers sold, which increased demand for everyone. However, dealers hated the low prices offered in the ads, which companies like Tower could offer, because they had an unfair pricing advantage—they were also wholesalers and didn't have to charge sales tax. To be competitive, dealers had to cut their margin down to the bone.

I told the sales team this would actually be good for dealers, because of the innovative method we were going to use. We would be the first in our industry to establish Minimum Advertised Pricing

(MAP), which would lead to higher margins for dealers. To further show our commitment to dealers, we promised that Horizon Hobby would not sell to consumers directly for anything less than the MAP price. Dealers could, but we wouldn't.

In addition, Horizon would bombard the marketplace with catalogs and magazine ads through our mail-order division to create demand for Horizon brands. It was the best of mail order (heavy advertising) without the worst of mail order (heavily discounted prices.) In fact, MAPs would create more margin for them than they could get selling other brands.

I got through my presentation and answered every question thoroughly. Slowly, the shock wore off and Lisa, one of our star salespeople, said, "We don't know how this is going to work, Rick, but if you say it will, we'll give it a try, because we trust you." That was huge. She was a veteran and her statement set the tone for the whole team to leave the room with hope and determination. I was gratified by their unequivocal support, but it sure put the pressure on. I had to make this strategy work!

A Winning Strategy

The dealer response was similar to that of our sales team, as I expected. They were shocked Horizon would do this. Some were angry and not afraid to express it. They said we were deserting them, breaking our promises, and actually worse than Hobbico, because at least Hobbico was honest about its conflict of interest!

I was making calls to key customers alongside the salespeople, so I heard the push back firsthand, and the disappointment in their voices dug deep. These dealers were our friends; we had close relationships with many of them. They believed in us, and thought Horizon was special. I knew it would be hard for them to visualize a mail-order company that could actually be good for them, but I naively thought they would be nicer to us.

We made hundreds of personal calls that day. Everyone was instructed to hold nothing back when it came to why we were doing this and how it would affect them. By getting ahead of the story, we held their trust for the most part, but used up a lot of social capital in the process. In the end, most dealers said the same thing our sales team had said, "I don't know how this is going to work, Rick, but if you say it will, I'll give you a chance to prove it."

It should be noted that just like when we bought HD, we had written in great detail the explanation for the change along with a Q & A sheet for the sales department to use. Honest, direct, and consistent communication resolves a lot of issues in advance and inspires trust. This is true in business and it's true in personal situations. Letting the story get written by others who have limited knowledge leads to painful misunderstandings. Important issues have to be faced head-on.

Over the next two years, we created a new kind of mail-order company, transitioning the company we bought (Indy R/C) from a discount mail-order house into a Horizon marketing tool to stimulate demand for our brands. We created a beautiful catalog of Horizon brands, much like what was common in Europe and Japan. It told a story about each product that gave it a certain charm or character, making each one more interesting to modelers. We built an easy-to-use website in the same manner. Consumers loved it, because they had so much more information about the products. We encouraged them to get the product at their local hobby shop, but they could always get it easily and quickly from us if they didn't have a good retailer nearby.

Amazingly, we didn't miss a beat. Our strategy was sound—demand for Horizon brands grew and we kept our word to dealers by improving their margins. The mail-order division positioned us well for the coming years. Not only did we now have a method of holding the sale, even when a dealer didn't promote our products, but we developed a robust online presence that was key to our success when buying online became the norm.

We also became more attractive to manufacturers around the world, since our distribution model included direct retail sales. However, foreign hobby companies wanted us as their marketer and distributor for North America only. They already had tight bonds with distributors in Europe, Asia, and other parts of the world. Yet, our advertising now transcended the US and we weren't getting the benefit of the international demand created for our exclusive brands. We started setting our sights on the rest of the world.

Rebirth

As I look back over the history of Horizon, I realize that every five to eight years, we needed a significant change in our business model in order to optimize the business. Being open to changes in strategy was crucial. Each one was risky, and somewhat difficult. But, without those painful "rebirths," Horizon would never have experienced the growth and success we had.

We started Horizon as a pure distributor in 1985. In 1992, we changed our business model drastically by acquiring exclusive brands. In 1998, we did it again by going consumer direct. Now, in 2004, we were experiencing another rebirth—developing an in-house team of engineers to design innovative, easy-to-use products from the ground up that would broaden the audience for R/C hobbies and allow us to sell them worldwide.

Each one of Horizon's rebirths came out of bi-annual strategic planning retreats.

Beginning in 1987 and every two years thereafter, we took all of our senior managers offsite for a planning retreat. For three days, we would pause to re-evaluate our company and set objectives for the coming two years. We always started by revisiting our vision, mission, and values to see if we wanted to tweak or change them. Next, we would honestly, often harshly, analyze our strengths, weaknesses, threats, and opportunities. From this analysis we set objectives to take full advantage of the opportunities before us.

I viewed these strategic planning retreats as one of my most important responsibilities. They reinforced the significance of our three values (the Golden Rule, Customer Is Boss, and Servant Leadership), prioritized key objectives for the coming two years, and made sure everyone was working from the same playbook. We included spouses and planned fun events for them while we were in meetings, to show we also valued their commitment to Horizon. It was a mind-expanding, team-building, enjoyable getaway that made our people feel special, important, and involved.

In hindsight, I have to say that this practice—and the emphasis on these values—were a significant reason that Horizon Hobby became the success story it did. The retreats provided concentrated opportunities to develop a culture that would embody the company. These values were our highest priority, even higher than the bottom-line profit.

The retreats also gave me, as the leader, an opportunity outside of the fast-paced, task-oriented work environment to invest personally in my team, and work on the relational and "soft-skill" aspects of our company. This would be key if Horizon were to truly accomplish its mission, "to see the world impacted by God through the influence of Horizon and its people."

Servant Leadership

There are certain things a leader has to do to drive the culture, empower people, and get the most out of an organization. Some things just can't be delegated. For example, I could have planned the strategy for moving into mail order and internet sales and delegated the communication to someone else. However, I consider myself a strategic leader. Speaking directly to the sales team showed I cared for them personally and knew how important they were to Horizon. Making dealer calls alongside the sales team reinforced their belief that I would never ask them to do something I wouldn't be willing to do.

I've always believed I had a distinct advantage as the leader at Horizon, because I was not a modeler and knew so little about the products. It was easy for me to include others in decision-making and depend heavily on their knowledge, talent, and expertise. Often the leader is the expert and heavily invested in the products sold. But leading people and running a business with excellence is what I was heavily invested in—not the products themselves. My priority was genuinely loving people, providing resources for them to use their skills successfully, dreaming bigger than humanly possible, and achieving excellence in everything we did.

It was not unusual for visitors touring Horizon to ask, "What are you feeding these people? Everyone is so friendly, happy in their job, and totally committed to Horizon. It's like Pleasantville around here." Well, that wasn't exactly our main objective, but we knew that if our people felt respected and happy, our customers and vendors would be happy, and our sales would grow. Happy people make the world a better place, starting with our everyday work environment.

In the end, it came down to living our values, and reproducing them in our company culture—and that started with me and Larry. Because, when you are a leader, people are always watching, and what you do is a lot more important than what you say. They want to know who you really are—if you're genuine. Leaders sometimes write a strategic plan and then put it in a drawer, never to be looked at again. They put wonderful sounding values on the wall, but treat people like they don't matter. They write a mission statement that sounds like they're going to save the world, and then focus on profits for themselves or stockholders. We were determined that would not be us.

The Golden Rule.

Customer Is Boss.

Servant Leadership.

These were the priorities that mattered to me—and most importantly Servant Leadership. In this model of leadership, the company org chart is inverted and looks like this: CEO at the bottom, who serves the VPs, who serve senior managers, who serve supervisors, who serve our frontline people, who serve our customers. The hands under each line demonstrate the support given those above the line by the person to whom they report.

A servant leader shares power, provides employees all they need to be successful, and helps people be the best they can be. A servant leader is not self-serving, but listens to others and attaches value to their ideas. A servant leader doesn't blame others, bring others down to make himself look better, or try to "beat" others. A servant leader wants to win as a team.

At the same time, a servant leader is still a LEADER. People need and want clear direction, knowledge of the plan, understanding of what their role is in the plan, and accountability. A servant leader doesn't slink around sheepishly, trying to make everyone happy. He or she holds people accountable and meets personnel issues head on, promptly. A servant leader understands the vision and how to achieve it. He or she is able to inspire people to follow him or her. A servant leader is always prepared, trustworthy, caring, and honest.

In his book *Servant Leadership*, Robert Greenleaf (considered to be the father of the servant leadership movement) states, "The great leader is seen as *servant first*, and that simple fact is the key to his greatness." He goes on to say a servant leader begins with the natural feeling that one wants to serve others. Then it's a conscious choice to aspire to lead. One who is a *leader first* feels the need to begin by assuaging power to accomplish his goals. For him it is a later choice to serve—after leadership is established.

A great example of a servant leader is found in a little-known book in the Old Testament. Nehemiah is a powerful story about how a person just like you or me approached his role in the saving of a nation. When he discovered his people were in need, Nehemiah exhibited all the characteristics of a great servant leader. He was compassionate, genuinely wanted to serve first, felt called to lead, was a visionary, created a strategy to achieve his vision, stayed on mission though opposed mightily (by those outside and in), had a bias for action, was a succession planner, and celebrated victories.

Nehemiah is my favorite book on leadership, and it's largely because he was just a regular guy. I believe Jesus is the best leader of all time, considering His vision is still being carried out two thousand years after His death and resurrection! He was a servant leader like no one else (see Philippians 2:5-8). But, I love to use the thirteen chapters of Nehemiah as a training manual for would-be leaders, because it paints a picture in compact form of a leader I can better identify with. Jesus is the model, but He had that "perfect" thing going for Him.

People don't want to be managed. They want to be led. And they want to be led by a great leader. One of the great tragedies in life is there are so few great leaders. We created a position at Horizon for a person whose sole responsibility was to make sure everyone was reporting to a great leader. He did a great job training our leaders and supervisors, but we found that servant leadership is a hard thing to teach. The force behind the authority of a servant leader is leading by example. If one doesn't start with the motivation to serve others first, it's not likely they will become a servant leader.

I believe servant leadership was the key driver at Horizon. Everything seen on our wallet card was important, but teaching, modeling, and expecting our leaders to act as servant leaders was the ingredient that led to financial success at Horizon. It gave people the confidence to carry their success beyond the workplace to home and at play. We weren't perfect, but we had enough leaders serving others for it to become part of our DNA.

9

Ultimate Faith

Meanwhile, God was poised to do something significant in the Stephens family that would dramatically affect the trajectory of our lives. I remember it beginning when Jeanene and I were driving along the 405 in Los Angeles on the way to a play. Jill (our oldest daughter) and Matt (her boyfriend) were in the back seat of our rental car. They hadn't been dating very long, but Jill seemed to really like this young man, so we wanted to learn more about him. Our conversation was rolling along nicely when Matt brought up how much Josh McDowell's book, *More Than A Carpenter*, had meant to him. He had read it in high school and told us, "That's when I fell in love with Jesus." Our hearts melted. I immediately thanked God for bringing this young man into my daughter's life. I knew he could very well be "the one" for her.

Jill had moved to Pasadena after grad school and taken a job as a speech pathologist in the schools there. She met Matt through her roommate, who was a classmate of his at Fuller Theological Seminary. Jeanene and I loved this adventure Jill was experiencing as she began her career, and we certainly enjoyed visiting her in the Golden State. It didn't take long for her to settle in and adjust to life as a Californian.

One thing I learned from our very first experience with a daughter leaving home and nearing marriage is that it's a very weird feeling.

Neither Matt nor I knew how to act about the fact that both of us loved the same woman! Our relationship was tentative and on unsure footing at first, but I soon accepted the fact that this young man was going to take over my role as Jill's protector and become the most important man in her life. It was emotional to relinquish my standing.

Their courtship was short. Soon after we returned to Illinois, Matt and Jill got on the phone together to tell us they were getting married on July 8th—of that very same year. It was only four months away! They said they had it all figured out and wanted the wedding to be in the Chapel at Snowmass, Colorado, where we had vacationed for so many years. We were surprised at the speed of the process, but got on board quickly. Together with Jill and Matt, we hurriedly put together wedding plans that would make for a wonderful experience.

We got to know Matt much better during the planning phase and had a great time together. The food tasting for the reception was especially meaningful. We were to go to the restaurant on top of Aspen Mountain where the reception would be held, but it was snowing and windy that day so the gondola was closed sporadically. Getting to our tasting party was going to be a challenge. Finally, there was a short break in the weather and the gondola re-opened. Was it an act of God or just the way it happened?

It turned out to be an unforgettable experience, so I'll go with the act of God. We laughed and talked over wine while we enjoyed the delicious choices of food for the wedding reception, with huge snowflakes continuing to blanket the mountain outside. It was an intimate experience for just the four of us. But, by the time our party ended, the lifts were no longer running and everyone was gone. The only way down was on a snowmobile or Sno-Cat. Matt and Jill jumped at the chance to ride down on snowmobiles. Jeanene and I took the Sno-Cat. What a ride! It was one of the best days we ever had with Matt.

At the time, Matt was busy as a youth pastor at a church near Oceanside, California, and didn't care to have a lot of input on the wedding, but there were a few things he felt very strongly about. One was that he wanted to walk with Jill down the aisle. To be honest, I was crushed! I was so looking forward to the experience of walking my daughter down the aisle—but ultimately, I resigned myself to the fact that it was all part of letting go and moved on. However, Matt and Jill knew how disappointed I was, and, at the last minute, changed their minds. It was all part of the healthy tension our family felt as the first new member was joining us since Marnie was born twenty years earlier. We were learning to work through the changes and adjustments as a family.

Activities were planned for the entire week of the wedding for those who wanted to make a vacation out of it, and many did. There was Jeeping on the mountain, hiking, fishing, golf, and all the things we love about Colorado. Jill and Matt made a terrific couple and it was a wonderful week of fun and celebration.

Tragedy Strikes

It was one year later (almost to the day) that I was in Galena, Illinois for an FCA National Board meeting when I received a frantic call from Jill. Doctors had earlier discovered a cyst on Matt's back and this was the day of surgery to remove it. We didn't think it was a big deal . . . but it was. Crying into the phone, Jill explained that during the surgery, doctors had discovered a terrible cancer, angiosarcoma, which had spread extensively.

Matt and Jill had just built a new house in Oceanside. They both loved their jobs and had such a bright future together. This kind of thing was not supposed to happen! My little girl couldn't stop sobbing and I was two thousand miles away, unable to console her.

I had ridden my Harley Davidson (my hobby for forty-five years) to Galena for the FCA meetings. It was a somber, slow ride home along the Mississippi River as I tried to grasp what was happening. Jeanene and I changed all our plans for the next week so we could go to California. Marnie had just had tonsillectomy surgery and needed Jeanene's help, so I left alone on the first flight out. Jeanene was set to join me a few days later.

Jeanene left according to plan, but on the way to the airport got word that Marnie's stitches had broken and she was bleeding profusely. Boy, when it rains, it pours! Jeanene returned home to care for Marnie and we were on the phone a lot that week.

Matt's prognosis was not good—the doctors basically told us there wasn't much they could do for him. We offered to use all the resources within our power to see if there might be something that someone, somewhere, could do. It was not an easy call for the young newlyweds to make. They could either search and travel far away for the best care possible, or they could stay at home and focus on the quality of life Matt had left. Matt showed grit and determination by electing to make his full-time job beating this cancer. After using the YPO Health Network to research options, Matt elected to go to MD Anderson in Houston.

The next year was difficult as we navigated the health system, dealt with Matt's chronic pain, tried different chemotherapies, and managed a variety of potent drugs—all while trying to live life to the fullest in the midst of strife. Matt was in charge. Jill did everything that needed to be done for him and she was great at it. Jeanene and I could only provide support. We believed our main job was to make life for them as pleasant as possible during the process, even though Matt and Jill had been dealt such a hard hand.

Matt's faith was strong. He fought cancer courageously while remaining true to God. Every single day, he looked for how God might be using his illness to draw others into a closer relationship with Him! Our entire family was transformed because of Matt's faith. And Matt became my mentor during this raw and emotional time. He was intentional about sharing his life and death with me during that year of illness. It was as if God called him to help me, even though he was the one who was sick. As a result, much of how I view life and death today is because of him.

At the beginning, Matt and Jill (nicknamed Milt) needed to stay in Houston for several months as Matt received treatment. Miraculously, some friends of ours knew a professor who taught at MD Anderson Cancer Center. He and his wife sometimes took young patients like Matt into their home, and they did that for the two of them. This made life much more pleasant for Milt during this time of intensive chemotherapy. It was a blessing and provided comfort during such turmoil.

Jeanene and I spent as much time as we could in Houston with Milt. After a few months, the doctors prescribed a chemo that could be administered by oncologists in California, so they were able to return home to Oceanside. We all had a job there. Matt was the leader, the "CEO"—it was his vision we all followed. Jill was in charge of "Operations"—she kept the schedule of appointments, watched over the taking of drugs, tussled with the doctors and hospitals, navigated the health insurance quagmire, and took care of Matt for the most part.

Jeanene was the "Communications Director." Friends and family were calling often to find out how Matt was doing. It was emotional and time consuming to give the update over and over, even though we knew everyone had the best intentions. So, Jeanene and Matt came up with an idea.

When Matt was first diagnosed, Jeanene wrote an email to a small group of friends to answer their questions and update them on how everyone was doing. Matt was so impressed by what she had written and the response received from people, he decided this might be more than a way to keep people informed—it could become a ministry to help others. He gave Jeanene freedom to share how faith can be lived out even in the midst of this ultimate experience. How amazing that most of his thoughts remained about others.

Jeanene began sending a "Matt Update" regularly to a few friends. People were inspired by her words and passed them along to others. Eventually hundreds were reading her Matt Updates and praying for our family, some of whom we didn't know and would never meet. This was just one of the ways Matt saw God touch lives through his illness.

My job was to be Matt's "Personal Assistant." I did whatever was needed to make his life more comfortable. I was always on call and hopped on a plane at a moment's notice if I could do anything to help.

Through It All, God Is Still Good

My big opportunity came when Matt could no longer read his Bible himself, and I had the extraordinary privilege of reading it to him. It started off casually, but then I became more intentional, searching for stories and meditations from history that related to Matt's position. We read how men and women dealt with loss, going all the way back to Abraham, including David and Jesus and their experiences with suffering. We read about how sometimes Jesus healed, and sometimes he did not. No matter what, God was always close by to comfort and guide people through their most difficult times of life.

How wonderful were those quiet, peaceful times when I would read to Matt. I loved sitting at his bedside reading his Father's words to him. Both of us knew he was nearing the most personal and special of all times, when he would leave this earth and see Jesus face to face. What an honor it was for him to give me a front row seat. Passages from Psalm, John, and Revelation 21 took on special meaning for us both as we read together.

Matt fought hard, but every time we felt some hope, the air would get knocked out of us with the next doctor's report. I remember so many times when we heard bad news, Matt would ask for some time alone. I believe he used those moments to be alone with God, process the news, pray, and put it in perspective. It was never long before he would invite Jill or all of us back into his hospital room. Then he would seem to take on the job of comforting us! He loved the Lord and knew God was using him in a big way. We were all strengthened by Matt.

Saying Good-bye

On July 3rd, 2002, Jeanene and I were at a movie in Aspen with friends when I received a call from Jill. All the doctors were now telling her there wasn't anything more they could do for Matt except keep him comfortable. It wasn't a surprise, and yet it was heavy on my heart as I heard the words come out of her mouth. I was devastated.

We took a charter to California the next day. We didn't know how long Matt had on this earth, so we rented a condo in Carlsbad for three months in order to be with them the whole time. We wanted to be near the ocean, partly for our comfort and partly because Matt loved the beach—he and Jill could spend time with us there. We were in California most of July, August, and September.

Life gets really hard sometimes. It doesn't get harder than this.

One thing Matt taught me was that death is simply a part of life. None of us escape it. Most have eighty years or more, but some, like Matt, have far fewer. Either way, our physical life on Earth is no more than a tiny dot on the long line of our spiritual life with God.

Matt died physically and moved on spiritually to be with God on August 11th, 2002. He was alert, engaged, and thinking about Jill, his parents, his sister, and everyone he was leaving behind, until the last week of his life. He slept restlessly the last week, unaware of his surroundings. It was agonizing to see him in such discomfort during those final days. But, God's timing is perfect. When it was time for Matt to go . . . he went.

One of us was always at his bedside. It was obviously devastating for Jill and we wanted for her to somehow feel better. We finally convinced her she needed a break from caring for Matt, so she went to a friend's house to sit in their hot tub. She had barely entered the hot tub when Matt passed. It was as if he needed to know she would be able to move on with her life before he would leave. This was the first time she had stepped away in months. Maybe it showed Matt she was going to be okay.

I've heard people say, "Death is not so bad, but I hate the thought of dying." I believe this is true in that once I leave this earth and become familiar with the next stage of life with God, I will be more than fine! But the process of leaving this world is really hard physically and unnerving emotionally. We naturally become anxious and afraid when faced with uncertainty, and death is the ultimate uncertainty.

Yet, one of the most often repeated phrases in the Bible is, "Do not be afraid." I believe God is telling me, *I know you can't see into the future but I can, and it will be okay. I created you and know what I'm doing. You can depend on the fact that I've got the next stage of your life all taken care of.*

The only way I know to counteract the ultimate uncertainty is through ultimate faith. Joy and victory can't be experienced fully without pain and loss. The worst of times leads us to dig deeply and we see life at its barest. When we accept there is a bigger picture than what man sees and God is in control of it all, we have the kind of faith Matt demonstrated and I strive for—ultimate faith.

In Memorial

Some young friends of the family who came to California for Matt's service were runners. They and some other friends had decided to run the Chicago marathon to raise money for cancer research in Matt's name. Though the marathon was only six weeks away, I was so inspired that I decided to join them. I ran six miles regularly, but marathons require a lot more training than a mere six miles. However, I felt this was special and believed I could do it. I ran longer distances for the next three weeks and then "tapered" for three weeks. I was ready.

A big group came to Chicago to cheer us on and I felt Matt's spirit with me that day. The weather was perfect on a cold October morning. I ran the only marathon I ever ran in four hours, twenty minutes, averaging ten-minute miles—exactly my goal. It was totally unnatural for me to be able to do that! I can't help but believe Matt ran with me. It was an exhilarating, spiritual experience.

The years of 2001 to 2003 were a deep valley for our family. It felt like a very long time. However, our attitude was always to make the best of life, even in the midst of difficult and painful events. Whether it's family or career, bad things happen and good things happen. We must accept both in stride. The trick is to find ways to enjoy life—and each other—when disaster strikes, and not get too carried away when things break in our favor. Life is never as bad as it seems when in the valley, nor as good as it seems at other times.

There is a happy ending to this story. Jill met a wonderful man (Mike) whom she married in October of 2004. She could not have found a better husband and father, nor one more understanding of her first love. Then Lars was born, then Steffen, and Hans. Our family will always remember and love Matt, but we also love Mike and the life he has created for Jill and their boys.

10

Navigating Success

During Matt's illness, Horizon's reputation as a responsible leader in the industry grew. We continued changing our business model to better align with where we believed the industry was going. We were flexible. Adaptive. There was no denying we were the company to watch as our sphere of influence broadened. Our willingness to take risks with new methods and products turned Horizon into a driving force that others depended on to grow the entire market.

Everything we did was designed to be of the highest quality— personal relationships, our customer service, and our products. Our motto internally was, "You might pay a little more at Horizon, but it's worth it!" Hobbico owned the market when it came to wide selection and low price. We had to set ourselves apart, and we did so by becoming known for superb quality in everything we did. It was a strategy we stayed with through the years and it exploded in 2004 with the advent of 2.4GHz spread spectrum radios.

Innovating

Since 2001, an inventor from Silicon Valley, Paul Beard, had been working on a way for R/C radios to operate without interference from other radios and electronic systems. Paul believed that the spread spectrum technology (2.4 GHz) used in cell phones could be adapted to R/C radios. Up to this time, the number of frequencies available to the hobby market was limited by FAA regulations. Crashes occurred far too often due to interference from other radios on the same channel—basically, there were too many R/C radios trying to use the same frequency. However, 2.4 GHz would eliminate that problem for modelers. It could be huge!

Our in-house genius, Eric, met Paul at a flying field event and thought his idea had tremendous potential. Eric tried to sell us on the idea of hiring Paul to develop this technology, but our product development department was skeptical. They agreed it would be a huge benefit to modelers, but developing a radio system from scratch was outside everyone's comfort zones. Everyone . . . except for Eric. This was an idea that had enormous potential, but looked impossible to achieve. These were the kinds of ideas that Eric and I loved.

We hired Paul as Vice President of Engineering in 2004. It required a large investment to pull him away from his own business of developing computer and telecommunications systems in San Jose, California, but Eric thought Paul was close to bringing the concept to market, and that it could turn the industry upside down. Paul remained in California and worked with Eric to perfect the technology for the R/C marketplace. And then, the fireworks started.

By this time, JR Radios had become our largest supplier, nearing Futaba in sales in the US. JR's high-quality manufacturing, along with Eric's guidance to design radios with unique features for US modelers, had worked well over the past twelve years. We were now committed to creating a new radio line with 2.4GHz, but we didn't want to compete with JR, not to mention the fact that we had no expertise in manufacturing.

With the concept nearing completion, we took the new technology to JR, explained the magnitude of the invention, and urged them to become partners with us by using our Intellectual Property (IP) in JR radios for worldwide distribution. We would get a share of the profits from worldwide sales in return for their use of the technology our team had come up with.

JR considered this carefully but, for a variety of reasons, turned us down. What it came down to was this: although what Horizon was offering might be groundbreaking, it made them uncomfortable to be so nonconforming in a very competitive landscape. This was a huge setback, leaving us few options. The learning curve to manufacture a high-quality radio line from scratch was steep, and competing with our anchor supplier would be painful (we'd been there before!). The only alternative was to ask JR if they would manufacture a radio line for us under a different brand name, but this was a long shot. Why would they help us develop a competitive line to their own?

JR considered themselves to be first and foremost a designer and developer of radios and electronic accessories—the manufacturing of them was a secondary function. This was our opening. We told them we would take the risk of this new technology, do all the design, development, and marketing work ourselves, and JR would simply be our exclusive original equipment manufacturer (OEM). They didn't have to take any risk. If we were successful, they would get a cut of the pie as the OEM manufacturer. They agreed!

We were ecstatic! We promised to design the new Horizon line of radios to look very different than JR radios, use 2.4GHz *only* in our systems (no other frequencies), and expect nothing more from JR than to manufacture the systems according to our specifications. We believed we could successfully promote our radios alongside JR because of the distinct differences. In the beginning, that was true, but little did we know what was about to transpire.

Fireworks

Eric and Paul named the new line Spektrum. JR produced a complete line of radio transmitters, servos, receivers, and accessories for Horizon under this new brand name. We marketed Spektrum as a radio without danger of interference. We demonstrated that a hundred modelers could all be flying at the same flying field at the same time and no one would get shot down or crash! It was brand new, exciting, and the market loved it. Though costly for modelers to change over radio equipment, early adopters did so immediately and the momentum grew. Spektrum became so popular we couldn't keep up with the demand.

This innovation catapulted Horizon into becoming a worldwide leader in the hobby industry. Futaba and the other radio manufacturers quickly went to work developing their own 2.4GHz technology, but it was not an easy thing to perfect and we had patents on our designs. For several years, we had the corner on the market, because every modeler wanted the security of 2.4GHz transmitters. We blew by two hundred million dollars in revenues and our profits soared.

During this time, we were hiring more engineers and designers to create new inventions across all R/C categories. Some developed methods to lengthen the power and life of batteries to improve electric flight, eliminating the messiness of gas engines. Others developed innovative systems to stabilize aircraft, making it simple for even beginners to fly them. New, easy-to-fly quad helicopters (the forerunners of drones) could be used indoors or outdoors and were a huge hit for Horizon. We released winners over and over again. Horizon had worldwide rights for these new products, since they were developed in house. As international demand for Horizon brands grew, we had remade ourselves once again.

Since the inception of Horizon, we had held a company-wide meeting at the end of every quarter. We would share our financial performance and reward employees by handing out a bonus check to everyone based on our profits. We also gave awards to Horizon employees who did something extraordinary for a customer, vendor, another employee, or the community—something that demonstrated one of our values in action.

These meetings were our way of reminding people that every person in the company was just as important as any other, and our success depended on everyone fulfilling their role with passion and excellence. The bonus checks they came to rely on put our money where our mouth was. I often would give God credit as our "ultimate CEO," and express my heartfelt gratitude to all Horizonites for making our vision a reality. I knew I wasn't smart enough to have pulled this off without them.

One day in 2005, I remember standing up in a quarterly meeting, having shared more record-shattering results and saying something I never thought I'd say. I said, "You all have done such an outstanding job that Horizon is now a world leader in this R/C industry. We may not be the largest, but we are the one driving the market for everyone else. What you have accomplished is nothing short of remarkable." It felt really weird saying this out loud. It sounded more boastful than my normal MO, but I believed it and wanted our people to know their hard work had paid off. God had performed such an unbelievable miracle through all of us in the past twenty years, I wanted it to be celebrated.

At the same time, I wanted people to understand that as the leader, we had a new role to fulfill, and it was sobering for those who grasped it. Now, the entire market depended on Horizon leading, and leading well. It was more important than ever that we innovate and create new products that would grow consumer demand, promote the hobby, and expand in a way that's best for the marketplace as a whole. So, it was a celebration, as well as a call to action.

Giving Back

Along with Horizon's success, the Stephens' personal financial statement was growing. Until the late '90s, we had remained very much in line financially with most of our social circle. In the early 2000s, this began to change. Our friends were happy for us, but we noticed that some others began to treat us differently.

Everyone loves to pull for the underdog, so for fifteen years it was a non-issue. But, when our success became more visible, we began noticing some people becoming more distant and untrusting. It's as if they were asking themselves, *Why him and not me? I work as hard as he does, if not harder. He's not even that smart. His parents or someone must have helped him get to where he is.* It's human nature to entertain such thoughts, and we felt a certain awkwardness grow among some acquaintances.

At first, Jeanene and I were asking similar questions about ourselves and felt guilty about what we had. We knew we didn't deserve it any more than anyone else and weren't sure why God had blessed us with such abundance. But, in 2000, Jeanene took a class at church at which our pastor, Phil Reed, said something that put us on a new pathway. During the class, someone asked what our role as the Church should be regarding hot-button social issues. Phil didn't answer the question directly. After a short pause, he said, "There's very little in the Bible that deals directly with these social issues, but there are more than six hundred verses that tell us to give to the poor, the needy, destitute, disenfranchised, powerless, and poor in spirit. If we love the 'least of these brothers of mine', the rest will take care of itself."

This had a lasting impact on Jeanene and we discussed it often. Giving generously made us feel like maybe the reason God had blessed us financially is so we could bless others. We never again had any trouble giving 10 percent of our personal income away and our guilt of having more than others disappeared with the giving. We felt enormously blessed that we got to keep 90 percent of what He had provided!

A few years later, Jeanene had the bright idea that we should also give 10 percent of Horizon's income to those in need. This caught me by surprise. If she had suggested it in the '90s when Horizon profits were slim, I could have agreed easily. But Horizon was much more profitable now, so 10 percent meant giving away a serious amount of money each year! I didn't even know if that would be fair to Horizon stakeholders. Shouldn't it be up to those who benefitted financially from Horizon to make those decisions themselves? However, deep down I knew she was right, and we began tithing Horizon's income.

Tithing both personally and corporately gave us the confidence to not worry about what others thought. We knew we were doing what God had led us to do with the money and that was all that mattered. If an acquaintance could not get past us being in a different tax bracket, that was their problem, not ours. We were still the same people we were before Horizon's success. It was a surprisingly refreshing and freeing stance to take.

I've found that giving is the antidote to self-centeredness and a lot of other things in life I don't want to be. Self-centeredness leads to self-pity, shame, guilt, stress, and chaos. It can also lead to pride, selfishness, false confidence, hoarding, and feelings of power over others. The very act of giving takes my eyes off myself and puts them on others. It forces me to think about another person and look at life from their point of view. It helps me look at life differently and better understand the many things I have to be thankful for—blessings that we can easily take for granted. Giving leads to contentment.

I was concerned at first that giving so much of Horizon's income versus reinvesting it would be a problem, but I was actually quite surprised at the results. Instead of hampering our growth, Horizon profits continued to increase. The next eight years were the most profitable of all Horizon's years in business.

It's interesting for me to look back at events related to giving and how they prepared me for this time of my life. I remember the anonymous gift that was just the right amount for a new transport van at Maranatha Bible Camp in 1967. And, when on the prayer team for Youth for Christ in 1972, I saw out of the corner of my eye Bill Anderson give several hundred-dollar bills to a staff member who could barely make ends meet. These experiences set the stage for me. God was laying groundwork early in my life to show me the blessings that come from giving generously.

Jeremiah 29:11 seemed to be following me around—"'For I know the plans I have for you,' declares the Lord, 'plans to prosper you and not to harm you; plans to give you hope and a future.'" It sure felt like God's plan for me was clear to Him from the beginning. He knew what decisions I would be faced with (both big and small) and which path I would take.

A More Abundant Life

Humankind is the only created thing able to experience the inner joy and peace that comes from unselfishness. We're the only part of creation with the ability to have inner thoughts, emotions, feelings of love, a spirit life, and a relationship with the Creator. Yet, our physical nature is all about self-preservation. We are naturally inclined to be devoted to ourselves, concerned with our own interests, and focused on our needs and pleasure. It's the natural makeup of every living thing.

Comparatively, generosity is the opposite of being devoted to oneself. I would argue the extent of one's generosity actually defines the extent of one's ability to live abundantly. Feeding our own pleasures and desires with more money, power, or material things of the world only leads to a dead end. Those things are ultimately unsatisfying and will never make us truly happy.

The quality of generosity replaces, forces out, and eliminates selfishness in equal proportion. A true sense of generosity is all that allows us to love God and love others, which Jesus said all the commandments boil down to. Generous people are able to experience abundant life. Without generosity, we are unable to let go of selfishness.

Jeanene and I have been abundantly blessed through the success of Horizon Hobby. We are beyond grateful for the comforts in this life we have been given, but we also know that what we have is only on loan to us while we're here on Earth. We will take nothing from this world with us except the love we feel in our hearts for others. The money, homes, cars, and "things" will all go back in the box for someone else to use when we "move" to Heaven.

We are humbled God has entrusted us with His resources. But, along with the resources come expectations. " . . . From everyone who has been given much, much will be demanded; and from the one who has been entrusted with much, much more will be asked."[6] We have a *responsibility* to invest wisely what God's given us and we take that seriously. Holding on tightly to His assets for our own use will not be applauded in either the physical world nor spirit world. No, our job is to actively use our time, money, and skills to gain an exceptional ROI in terms of helping those who are in need.

However, we are also comfortable using some for ourselves and believe that serves a purpose too. We don't feel guilt for having nice

---

6. Luke 12:4

things, as long as they are shared with others and don't interfere with giving to those in need. In one sense, they show others what is possible when you have a dream, go for it, and do it in a way that's pleasing to God. In another sense, living a life commensurate with success opens the door for relationships with successful people who may not otherwise have friends who love Jesus.

Money is at the root of a lot of evil, but can be used for a lot of good when stewarded well. Jeanene and I have received remarkable rewards from giving generously, to the point that we would be silly to not give. I don't understand it . . . except that God says it will happen that way.[7]

---

7. Malachi 3:10; Luke 6:38

11

Succession Planning

As early as the year 2000, I began to think about management succession. I owned two thirds of the company and Larry owned almost one third, with Jeanene's father still holding a sliver. We had bought my father's stock many years earlier as part of his estate planning.

I knew Horizon needed a structure to allow it to continue seamlessly, if something were to ever happen to me. I had established an advisory board (an outstanding group of four outside leaders plus Larry and me) in the early '90s, and we met quarterly like a real board, but the votes remained with Larry and me. Since I had the majority, my death would leave too much uncertainty for Horizon and my family. We needed a plan.

Conventional wisdom asserts that the first step in succession planning is to identify a leader who is ready to take over at any time. Janet was the first person I considered. My brother Larry was two years older than me, and Eric, though a genius, was not the right person for this job. Granted, Janet's degree in music didn't exactly qualify her for the job of president of the company, but she lived the values, loved what Horizon stood for, and was a great leader of people. I explained to her I believed she was the best person for the job, but that she needed more business background. If she would be willing to get her Executive MBA, we would pay for it and she'd be the next president of Horizon. She enrolled, but for family reasons could not continue. I agreed with her decision, but felt like I had to move on.

Today, I would probably look at this differently. History has shown me that having the right vision, values, and leadership ability is more important than understanding business, especially in a company like Horizon that puts values before anything else. Business skills can be taught; character cannot. In hindsight I believe that Horizon might have been better off with Janet in that role after me, even without the business training.

Brotherly Love

In mid-2001, when we learned Matt had cancer, Jeanene and I put everything else on hold to support him and Jill. Horizon needed a leader in my absence, so I asked Larry if he would be the interim president/CEO. I didn't know when I would be back full time. He said yes, just like he always did when I was in need.

Larry did an outstanding job while I was gone, but we bumped heads when I returned. I was back and acting like the CEO, even though Larry had the title. This led to some knockdown, drag-out confrontations that both of us hated. I was totally unfair to Larry, embarrassingly rude at times, and I made it clear I knew how to lead Horizon better than he did. I'm really not sure I was right. We have different strengths, but Larry is a great leader and he could have done it just as well. But, this wouldn't haven't solved the succession problem, since we were close to the same age and I wanted someone younger.

As the months wore on, our relationship grew more strained. Of course, neither of us wanted business to get in the way of our relationship, but I plowed ahead without thinking of the consequences. I was grieving and angry after Matt's death, and was more ambitious than ever to take Horizon to the next level. Finally, Larry did what very few people would have done. Though I had mistreated him as I forced my strategies on him, he humbly sacrificed his role out of love for God and love for me. Wow!

I learned later that he had prayed about it long and hard. Eventually, he felt like he heard a message that Horizon was my call from God, and his call from God was to help and support me. In other words, he believed God was telling him to take a back seat to his younger brother. Larry quietly gave up the role of President/CEO, but continued to do all he could to make me and Horizon successful. How many people would do that? My respect and love for this man could not be greater. He epitomized God's love for me in his actions.

New Leaders, New Owners

After this, we hired a series of young, bright leaders with succession in mind. One of these was a young man named Mike, whom we originally hired as Chief Information Officer. In time, he became President and did an outstanding job. Two years later Joe was recommended to us by a lifelong friend. Joe also was a great leader, someone who could help Mike in the short run, and another potential candidate to lead for the long haul.

This put Mike in a tough position. It was obvious Joe had strong leadership skills, and Mike knew he might also be a candidate for the job he wanted tremendously for himself. But, like me when I hired Eric at GP years before, he saw that Joe could contribute to the success of Horizon. So, in spite of the threat, he hired him as Vice President of Operations and the two became a great team. Horizon's leadership just became much stronger.

I've found that the best way to tell the quality of a leader is by the quality of the people he or she hires. Leaders who hire people as good as or better than themselves demonstrate healthy self-esteem and a desire to make the best choices for the organization, regardless of how it works out for them. Unfortunately, I have found most leaders to be more interested in protecting their turf, with self-interest as their key motivator. They are threatened by great leaders whose contributions might outshine their own, so they don't hire them. Hiring less capable people is a sure sign of a poor leader.

Now that we had two strong candidates for succession, I knew the question of stock ownership would come into play along with the change in leadership. Would we sell him our stock? Could the new leader accomplish a management buyout? Should we sell most of the stock to private equity, but continue to run it? Should we merge or sell to a strategic buyer in the marketplace? Should Larry and I retain ownership, retain the CEO title, and not worry about succession? We still had a lot of money invested in Horizon and the ROI on that investment would be out of our control if we gave up the lead.

One option we had been considering was a 100 percent Employee Stock Ownership Plan (ESOP). This involved a lot of government regulations and hoops to jump through, but it had its advantages. There were three primary factors that led us to an ESOP:

1. It allowed the family to take some money off the table, so our future didn't rely entirely on Horizon as we transferred the reins of leadership.
2. It allowed me to remain CEO and stay in control of the company as long as I wanted, while providing a seamless structure for the company if I were incapacitated for any reason.
3. It was an excellent mechanism to share the fruits of our labor with all our people—the very people who had as much to do with our success as I had.

This was a big decision in the life of Horizon, and would mark a true change of ownership from the Stephens family to all the people of Horizon. I liked the idea from the start, but didn't really know what to expect as we entered the world of government regulations. In many ways, a 100 percent ESOP is like becoming a public company on a smaller scale.

As individual owners, Larry and I had made decisions as needed with no one to answer to except God. We didn't want that to change as long as we were in the lead.

The ESOP structure is a strange animal and it took us almost two years to get fully comfortable with it. After a great deal of research, we learned we would retain full authority as long as we did not take advantage of employees to benefit ourselves. The only real difference was that from now on, our people were the ones to benefit from any increase in the company's value instead of the family. If we all did a great job, the value of each employee's share would grow and go into a retirement fund with their name on it.

The ESOP accomplished a lot of important goals for us, but it was not something we *needed* to do. Horizon was in the midst of a powerful growth curve. We were setting revenue and profit records every month, and all indicators pointed toward more of the same in the next few years. Financially, our family would be the recipient of that exploding growth if we retained ownership. The decision to sell 100 percent to the employees was based solely on what we believed God would have us do with His asset.

The Stephens family spent a lot of time praying for some kind of a sign that would show us which way to go. God had brought us this far; we certainly didn't want to make this big a decision without His confirmation. If things didn't line up, if it was too hard to execute, if it didn't accomplish all our goals, then we were more than ready to back off and retain ownership.

There were many obstacles to overcome. We needed to agree on the value of the stock, we needed assurances that would allow us to lead as we had in the past, and we needed to decide how much of the purchase the family would finance and how much would be borrowed. There were thousands of details in the transaction to sort through. We hired the most respected attorneys, appraisal firms, and trustee in the ESOP world and they were expensive. We wanted to be sure it was done in a way that was fair to both employees and the family.

For months, I went back and forth in my thinking about the ESOP, looking for confirmation or denial from God. One day I'd think it was a great idea, but the next, I'd want to leave things as they were. I spent many hours thinking, praying, evaluating, and running numbers. I was constantly trying to discern God's will. We were in an excellent negotiating position, because I was perfectly fine if the ESOP didn't work out. In fact, life would be much simpler without it and we would be far better off financially.

There were a number of times I was ready to throw in the towel. Each time an unacceptable provision was added to one of the agreements, I thought it might be a sign to pass on the ESOP. More than once I said, "That's it! The deal is off. We're staying as we are." But every time, the provision was removed or changed until I was left with no serious objections. I finally concluded the ESOP was the way to go.

A New Beginning

For me and my family, this was a big deal with a lot of money involved. Closing was set for September 15, 2006 at the offices of Morgan Lewis in Chicago. Jeanene's dad came up from Alabama for the closing with Larry and me. We entered a large conference room, maybe thirty by fifty feet, with a huge conference table and accompanying side table spanning the entire length of the room. Folders filled with documents awaiting signatures lined the side table from one end to the other. I couldn't even begin to count them all. Along with our attorneys from Morgan Lewis, there were attorneys representing the trustee and the lead banks. It took several hours to sign all the agreements, in the right order, but eventually . . . it was done.

Afterwards, we had a celebratory dinner with our attorneys and representatives in a private room at a beautiful restaurant on the Chicago River. Everyone was excited and happy, except Jeanene and me. Larry was excited because the weight of Horizon was lifted off his shoulders and he could retire. Jeanene's dad was happy because his investment of ten thousand dollars was paying off handsomely. All the attorneys and banks were happy, because they had billed millions of dollars for the transaction. But, Jeanene and I curiously didn't feel so much like celebrating. Unlike everyone else, nothing had really changed for us. Frankly, we had enough money before the transaction and the chance to make much more if we'd held onto Horizon. We had just capped our upside.

However, the weight of Horizon was still on our shoulders; we weren't retiring yet. The banks provided most of the debt, but Larry and I loaned a great deal of our proceeds from the transaction back to the company in the form of subordinated debt. If Horizon ran into financial trouble, the banks would get their money first and we would likely not get ours.

If that weren't enough, we were now responsible to our employees for Horizon's stock value to grow. The next day I would stand before them and explain what this could mean for them financially. But I knew that for it to ever become reality, I had to make sure Horizon performed well in the future. Horizonites couldn't lose anything, but without growth in company value, they would get nothing from being owners of Horizon.

It was a bittersweet moment for Jeanene and me. And there was no one we could talk to about it. It looked pretty darn good to everyone else! On the inside we felt like we had birthed and raised this "baby" for twenty-one years and it now belonged to everybody else. Yet, we were still responsible for its success.

The next day, I explained the change in ownership to all the Horizon employees. I wanted them to know that if we all acted like owners and Horizon continued to grow in value, it would mean a lot of money to every one of them. This is one of the selling points of an ESOP—that employees become highly motivated to do a great job since they own stock in the company. Though the rewards are long term, they now had the opportunity to get ahead financially in a big way.

After the meeting, it was simply back to work. We now had a structure that insured Horizon would live on seamlessly after me. Our advisory board became a real Board of Directors and Mike was doing a great job as President. He and I worked together well. I loved leading the culture while he executed the strategy.

Smooth Sailing

Horizon continued to prosper. We fed the market with more and more new and innovative products. In 2008, Mike led us in an acquisition of JSB, a distributor in Germany owned by a former fighter pilot and passionate modeler. He had grown JSB quickly as a distributor of Horizon brands in Europe (EU) and our businesses were closely intertwined. JSB was an ideal partner with which to merge and a way to take advantage of the second largest R/C marketplace in the world behind the US.

We built a 90,000-square-foot facility in Elmshorn (near Hamburg) to provide faster service to mainland Europe than we had been able to provide from Horizon Hobby UK in Harlow (near London). Horizon Hobby UK continued to expand the UK market while Horizon Hobby Deutschland became one of the largest hobby companies in all of Europe. We also opened a retail, sales, and engineering office in Shanghai to better communicate with our Chinese manufacturers and try to sell to Chinese modelers. Our original vision was "to see the world impacted by God through the influence of Horizon and its people." Little did I know in 1985 that God would actually make that happen!

Then I gave the title of CEO to Mike, leaving me only with the role of Chairman of the Board. It was a huge mistake.

I wasn't ready to turn over the leadership of Horizon. In some cases, a chairman is able to work closely with the CEO and continue to lead the company in strategy and culture. More often, the new CEO wants to lead the show and within a year, I believed this is what Mike wanted. I was cramping his ability to act as the CEO. I was in his way. Maybe finding a leader to succeed me wasn't what I wanted after all.

I stewed and prayed about this for months. Was it simply a matter of a founder not wanting to let go? Was I ever going to be able to let go? Was I holding on too long? Was God's plan for me to continue helping people through the platform of Horizon? Or did He have something else for me to do? I asked God for a sign. He miraculously brought it all to a head, unexpectedly.

I had many conversations with Mike about what I thought he was missing in the CEO role. He knew his job was in jeopardy. One day, at a working lunch, we were discussing a problem I thought needed to be fixed right away. Before I knew it, the truth was on the table: though he made a great president, I did not have confidence in his ability to be a CEO. Not surprisingly, he disagreed with my assessment, but he handled it very professionally.

A few years after leaving Horizon, Mike started his own company in the hobby market, leading me to believe he probably would have been a great CEO at Horizon if I'd left him alone. But, in time, I saw God's plan unfold and realized that his departure was a necessary piece of the puzzle.

Joe had done a great job as Vice President of Operations, so I suggested we now appoint him President. However, one of our board members took it a step further and suggested Joe should also be named CEO and a full member of the board from the start, because it would be hard for him to trust me after what had happened with Mike. I was hesitant, because I still wasn't ready to let go of Horizon (surprise, surprise), but he had a point. So, I carefully wrote a job description for CEO, leaving strategic planning and the culture of Horizon in my hands as chairman. Joe and the board agreed and it was done.

The next two years were awesome. Larry retired, for the most part, but remained involved in the big decisions. I had more free time than ever before. Joe, Larry, and I met every Monday to discuss Horizon. Joe came prepared with the pertinent issues he was facing, and we would give him advice and direction. Joe trusted our judgment.

This had always been my dream—to pass the reins to a great leader who would carry on the vision God had given me for Horizon while I stayed involved as a trusted advisor. But, in the fall of 2010, this idealistic picture began to fade. Joe really wanted to lead Horizon on his own and see what he could do without so much involvement from me and Larry. He had appreciated our advice and help during the past two years, but didn't think the weekly meetings were necessary any longer. He also believed it was time for him to lead strategic planning without us, or people would still think we had the last word.

This was hard for me to accept, but I figured if I were in his position, I'd want to run the show too. Maybe this was God's timing for

me to really let go. And so I did. I focused on my new grandchildren and enjoyed a slower pace of life.

The company continued to show strong growth, with revenues reaching $335 million by the fall of 2012. On the outside, my succession planning seemed to have been a huge success. However, a company's financials are a picture of the past; they lag actual performance by twelve to eighteen months. In early 2012 I began to see some cracks in the armor. I wasn't confident we were on the right track.

As any entrepreneur reading this knows, when you start an organization and run it for almost thirty years, you have a feel for what's going on deep inside the belly of a company that no one else understands. You can feel it when things aren't right . . . and I could feel that things were definitely not right.

12

Letting Go

I sensed there was trouble afoot, so I searched for ways I might be able to help Joe on his terms as problems began to appear. He did so many things right, but I thought I could help him resolve the issues before they showed up in the numbers. I wanted us to work together again like we had so successfully his first two years as CEO. However, he was not interested in going back.

This put me in a tough spot. I either needed to let Horizon go or jump back in with a very loud bang. If I overruled our CEO in order to make the decisions I thought were necessary, it would destroy everything he had accomplished over the past four years as the leader. I tried to listen for God's leading, because the decision to let go or jump in with both feet would hugely impact the rest of my life and that of Horizon Hobby.

It's Time

It's probably obvious by now, but I love to work. The day I find myself without an important project or meaningful purpose for any length of time is the day I will feel like my life on Earth is nearing completion. I cherish time spent with family and enjoy travel, fine food, golf, and having fun with friends. But, making something special happen that improves the lives of others is what drives me. If I was being called to let Horizon go, I needed to fill the void.

There's nothing I can find in the Bible saying that we should retire. In fact, there's a long list of characters who did their best work late in life. People like Abraham, Sarah, Aaron, Moses, Joshua, Caleb, Eli, Zacharias, Elizabeth, and John (who wrote Revelation) are just a few examples. Psalm 92:12-15 says,

> *"The righteous will flourish like a palm tree, they will grow like a cedar of Lebanon; planted in the house of the Lord, they will flourish in the courts of our God. **They will still bear fruit in old age, they will stay fresh and green**, proclaiming, 'The Lord is upright; he is my Rock, and there is no wickedness in him'"* (emphasis added).

When I first gave up the title of CEO in 2007, I began thinking, *It's time to remake myself!* I loved Horizon, what it stood for, and how it impacted lives positively. I loved the platform it gave me to influence others and, yes, I loved the identity it gave me. I had no reason to give it up, except I felt like God had something else in mind for me. *I really wanted to know what was next!*

I prayed regularly that God would make it clear to me. No answers. But then something dawned on me! I recalled how, in the past, remaking Horizon could always be linked to a strategic planning retreat— maybe I needed a *personal* strategic planning retreat for my own future.

So, in the spring of 2008, I decided to devote two weeks to a personal retreat of reading, prayer, fasting, and meditation. Each day I would get up early and leave the house for a bench on the beach, the chapel at Sanibel Community Church, the Bean (coffee shop), or wherever I could find privacy to read, pray, meditate, and talk with God. Fasting was new to me, but I did the best I could by eating as little as possible in order to better focus my thoughts on God.

I didn't feel at all alone during this time, because I imagined I was going to a meeting with God each day, just as I would meet with a friend. I imagined God to be sitting across the table or beside me on a bench. It was like He was a person I could talk with freely. He talked with me through His Word and I talked with Him through prayer.

There were lots of ideas running through my head these two weeks. Should I start another company? Mentor others who were starting their own companies? Devote myself to a particular ministry? Go to seminary? I worked hard at this little retreat, searching for an answer, but came away with nothing—or so I thought.

In the following weeks, a message started to take form in my head: *I don't want you to DO anything, Rick! I just want you to devote yourself to Me.* I felt like God was telling me that it doesn't matter *what* I do, because it's not about the "job." It's about my relationship with Him, putting Him first, living with Him moment by moment, and including Him in everything I do. It's about aligning myself with Him. My "job" is simply to follow His lead for each day. I felt Him tell me that if I devoted myself to Him, He would take it from there.

Fire Alarm

I was still trying to understand this and apply it four years later as Horizon's performance began to wane. My gut was still telling me it was time to let go of Horizon, but I felt like I knew just what to do to right the ship. I was itching to jump in! But I recalled the last two years of my time at RP when my gut was telling me to move on, and I waited too long. I didn't want to do that again.

Horizon had been missing projections consistently and Joe called me in early November 2012 to say we likely would not meet the covenant requirements for our loan agreement at the end of the quarter. He explained it was a temporary cash flow problem and minor in scope. He'd been on bank boards for decades and knew they would understand the short-term inventory problems we were experiencing.

This was not such a minor problem to me. In my opinion, it was a smoldering fire, and it was time to call the fire department. I jumped back in.

I immediately called Larry, because I needed his help to turn it around. I asked Larry, who loved being retired, if he would change all his plans for the winter and go back to work with me. He was caught off guard and didn't commit at once, but within five minutes called back to say that, for me, he'd do anything. So yes, he'd be back in the office in a few weeks.

I returned to Horizon right away and began asking questions. I went directly to the people I trusted on the front lines to find out what shape we were *really* in. Within a week, I had pieced together the facts and saw deeper problems than a temporary cash crunch. Research & Development had made big quantity commitments based on overzealous projections of new product sales, and the department was running roughshod over Purchasing, affecting the rest of the company. No one was holding R & D accountable.

The first weekly executive team meeting I attended in late November was an eye-opener. Everyone had excuses for why things were going wrong, but in my opinion, the core problems were never discussed. I shared what I had learned from talking to people during the previous week, described what I thought the real issues were, and laid out the steps I thought were necessary to correct the problems. I also promised we were *not* going to miss our loan covenants the following month.

After the meeting, our fairly new CIO (Chief Information Officer) pulled me aside to tell me how refreshing it was to finally face the

real problems. The executive team understood them, but didn't know what to do about them. Sometimes, we leaders think we need to do it all by ourselves, but the people on the front lines know a lot more than we give them credit for. Our job as leaders becomes easier if we trust our people and let them do what they do best.

Larry went to work on the visible problems at hand: R & D, purchasing, and inventory reduction. At the heart of it was the R&D manager. We had to replace him to restore confidence in our people that we cared about our values.

I focused on the financials and the strategy. We had lost our edge of introducing products that were truly innovative. Remember, we were the industry leader—no one else was feeding the market with innovative new products like we were. If we didn't foresee the next new widget to take the market by storm, the entire industry would suffer. Our recent releases were missing the mark and consumer interest was shifting to inexpensive drones.

Larry changed R & D leadership without losing suppliers and worked with sales and purchasing to move as much of the overstock as we could to create some cash. We invited Yu Tian of Helang Electronics Company in Shanghai, our biggest vendor, for a visit around Christmas. If we could delay payments to Tian just a few weeks, totaling about six million dollars, we would meet the loan covenants required for the fourth quarter and gain the time needed to get things in order.

Larry, Joe, and I met with Tian and candidly laid out our cash flow problem, along with what we had done in the past few weeks to remedy the situation. We needed to be honest with Tian to regain his trust. Thankfully, it worked. He was happy to help, which got us over the hump. We met our loan covenants at the end of December and our ratios were in good shape again by spring 2013.

And, honestly, it felt good to be back in the game again.

Overstepping

By this time, I had seriously overstepped my bounds as chairman and really forced the leadership issue. A company simply cannot have two leaders. Joe acknowledged there were problems he wished he had been able to fix more quickly, but that didn't mean he wanted to give up his role as CEO. He didn't think the other problems I saw were significant or anything he couldn't handle himself. He appreciated that Larry (especially) and I had helped him put out the fire, but felt he could take it from here.

At this point, I believed there were three options to keep Horizon on track:

1. Persuade Joe to accept my help. I could stay behind the scenes, and he would get all the credit, but Horizon would do better with the two of us working together, like we did from 2008 to 2010. But this was a big ask of a CEO.
2. Replace Joe, which meant I'd have to lead again until I hired and trained a new CEO. That would take years, plus I couldn't be sure I would be successful at it. In addition, my team of Eric, Larry, Janet, Roger, etc. was aging with me.
3. Sell the company.

I didn't like option two at all, so if the first option didn't work, I'd probably need to sell Horizon. Over the next few months, I continued to ask God for direction. It was still His company. I was open to whatever He had in mind. I just wanted to follow Him.

I tried to re-build my relationship with Joe, but it wasn't working. I went to a few members of the board informally to see if they could convince Joe that Horizon could be better if he and I worked together. We discussed it together, honestly and openly. In the end, it became apparent that with all things considered, the board believed I should give Joe more time. I needed to step back and let him lead.

That decision was the beginning of the end for me at Horizon.

I was now left only with option three, to sell the company, unless God surprised me and led me to become CEO again. The stars were aligning in the "sell" direction, but I continued to fight against it. I wanted to fix Horizon! I could do this! I could make it better. I just wanted to fix it.

It all came to a head in our next board meeting, February 24, 2013. I outlined the three options I had been considering and asked the board's advice. Option one was long gone now, and no one liked option two. In their opinions, we had worked too long on succession planning to throw it away and start over again. Long story short: the board believed Joe could turn Horizon around. He just needed more time.

I felt like God had spoken. I had wrestled with Him about this, because Horizon was "my baby." I'd started it from scratch, watched it grow far beyond my wildest dreams, and seen so many exciting and powerful miracles performed while leading it. And now it was suffering. But, I had come to believe that God had something else for me to do, that my long season of life with Horizon was over. There was another chapter of my life that He wanted to write. It was time for me to sell and move on.

It soon became apparent that my having an office at Horizon didn't give Joe the freedom he needed to lead, so the board kindly suggested I move out. In a sense, I had managed to get myself fired from my own company! I thought it was pretty funny, to be honest. I found another office a few miles away, which I love and continue to enjoy today.

Selling Again

The next ten months were devoted to the sale of Horizon. There weren't any viable options for strategic buyers in our small industry, so my plan was to contact several private equity (PE) firms as soon as I could and shoot to get the highest price for our employees.

My first step in the process was to make a short list of PE companies who had shown interest in the past. Then I started talking with friends who had gone through the process, or were familiar with the PE business. And, of course, I discussed it with Horizon board members. Greg in particular was a likely source of information, because he was on the board of a PE company in Chicago that I liked and a partner in a local PE firm, Armory Capital.

Surprisingly, Greg expressed an interest in using Armory Capital to buy Horizon and allowing Joe to own part of it. I hadn't considered Armory because Horizon was larger than the companies in their existing portfolio, and I didn't want business to interfere with my family's close friendship with Greg and his family. We had skied, golfed, motorcycled, and traveled the world together for forty years. I was confident we would remain friends but knew it would be hard to watch the purpose of Horizon change under the ownership of a friend. For our family, Horizon was a remarkable ministry. For a PE firm, it would become an asset designed to produce an excellent ROI for investors. If the buyer were more distant, it would be out of sight, out of mind.

On the other hand, it essentially would be a management buyout (i.e., management and private equity partnering to buy the company), and that had a nice ring to it. Horizon would end up in local hands and leadership would remain the same, eliminating that uncertainty for employees. In fact, with only one bidder, we could keep the entire process under wraps, avoiding months of angst for employees, customers, vendors, and the industry. And due diligence would go more smoothly because both Armory and Joe recognized that Horizon's potential far outweighed any current shortcomings. It wouldn't be my first choice, but it might be God's. So, we pursued it.

I had a conflict of interest, so one of our board members led the negotiations with Armory, along with a second private equity firm they brought in due to the size of the deal. Reaching agreement on price and terms was an arduous process made more difficult by the ESOP structure. But, finally, the details were finalized and the deal was done.

The sale of Horizon Hobby, Inc. closed January 17, 2014. Through the transaction, God blessed several Horizonites with over a million dollars, over three hundred with six-figure sums, and a few hundred more with something under one hundred thousand. The ESOP was a success. Horizon had been passed on; the people who believed in and trusted Larry and me for so long were paid handsomely; and the Stephens family got their money out of the company. In the end, our family received roughly half, and the employees the other half, if the proceeds from the ESOP sale in 2006 and this one were added together.

Jeanene and I didn't feel like celebrating when we sold to the ESOP, and we didn't feel like celebrating now as the last ties to Horizon were cut. But we were thankful. Our "Promised Land" had led to so many incredible miracles over the life of Horizon, including how it came to be owned by the family, the unbelievable way it started in just three months from our basement, the people who chose to join the team, the fabulous growth of the first five years, the way God kept me from making irreparable mistakes like selling to Futaba, the development of Spektrum radios and other innovations that enlarged the hobby market, and how all our employees shared in the fruits of their labor in the end. All this, I believe, was orchestrated by God.

Our company had also been a wonderful ministry. Some people accepted Christ for the first time, some grew much closer to God, some had opportunities to learn about God and hear from Him who might not have otherwise. Spiritual outcomes are not so easy to measure, but everyone who came in our door saw something different about Horizon and I like to think they saw the love of God in our people. Our vision had been fulfilled: "To see the world impacted by God through the influence of Horizon and its people."

I know Larry and I made a lot of mistakes. We're not the smartest guys in the world, but God clearly had a plan to use our company for His purposes. He brought just the right people to make up for our weaknesses and we knew enough to depend on them. For twenty-eight years, God guided us through the valleys and over the mountaintops, keeping His arms of protection around us the whole time. And when it was time to move on, He made it clear I needed to let go of "my baby" so I could embark on a new journey with Him.

A Sense of Satisfaction

There is no greater privilege than to be used by God to accomplish His purposes. What He requires of us is to stay connected to Him, living in dependence on His limitless resources. Then, He is able to work through us to transform and make better the lives of those around us. We are grateful that God showed His constant presence as we journeyed to our Promised Land.

I am happy to say Horizon Hobby remains very successful today. The hobby market continued to shrink after the sale, as did Horizon. However, Hobbico filed for bankruptcy four years after our sale and Joe led the negotiations to buy its assets, which left Horizon as the only big player in the industry. I walked out of the building after the infamous 2013 board meeting and, as is often the case with a former Founder/CEO, no one ever contacted me for advice. I have no idea what might have been possible if I had remained involved, but it doesn't matter. I felt called to leave Horizon and it was the right path for me and Horizon.

I noticed a slight change in our vision statement made shortly after the sale. It became, "To see the world impacted <u>for good</u> through the influence of Horizon and its people." It wasn't surprising, because a financial company wants to do "good things" for others. But, at the end of the day, they answer to shareholders. Larry and I didn't have that restriction. We believed we answered only to God. If we led Horizon as best we could in alignment with God's purposes, the rest would take care of itself. We could never remove God from our Vision and Values, because *He was the heartbeat of Horizon and we owed our success to Him.*

As I learned early in my career, the owner gets to set the vision. Horizon is different today, but it's a great company made up of exceptional people, many of whom we worked with closely for years. I'm pleased they are healthy and profitable, and proud to be part of their history. But God did have more for me to do.

13

Family Matters

It was a cool, wet morning in Athens, Ohio. Our youngest daughter, Marnie, had chosen Ohio University (OU) for her college career and we had just moved her into her dorm the day before. I went for an early jog in a light, somewhat dreary drizzle along the Hocking River. It was a special time, as I pondered our last child entering college, and thought about the season of life that was coming to a close.

Upon completing my run around this rolling town, I found myself back at the entrance gate to campus, in front of a beautiful limestone and brick arch. I was praying for Marnie and feeling a special closeness to God. Jeanene and I trusted our girls, and they were wonderful daughters, but we were still slightly concerned that OU was known as a "party school." As I stood there in the mist thinking about it, I said, "Father, I pray there will be a revival at OU while Marnie is here, and that she will be a part of it." The only explanation I have for saying that prayer is that it was a nudge from God. No such thought struck me when Jill and Carrie entered their schools. But, it did on this day in 1999, and I continued to pray the same prayer for the next four years.

Within a couple weeks of her first day at OU, Marnie met some girls from The Navigators and started going to meetings with them. Her association with The Navigators cast the mold for her college career. She not only had a great time at OU, but came into a closer relationship with God and helped others do the same.

One of those she influenced was a young man named Joel Bokelman. She met Joel the first week of her freshman year and they went on a journey together to learn who God is and experience His presence all around them. They were married in 2005, with their faith in Christ and love for others on full display. I'll never forget their wedding day.

I wonder what would have happened if I'd skipped that little prayer at OU. Would Marnie still have met those girls with The Navigators and grown in faith just as much? Would she have married Joel? Would there have been this marriage with Christ at the center?

Sometimes I have thought that prayer is awkward or unnecessary. It's so easy to skip, and it would have been my usual behavior to let that moment early in the morning at OU pass right on by. *Every little thing* doesn't need to be prayed about, right? But, experiences like these tell me God is listening and wants to be a part of every thought I have, big or small.

Praying for my family is perhaps the best thing I've done for them and the best thing I could ever do for them. But, during my career, I have learned that much more than prayer is required to be a good father, husband, and grandfather.

Shifting Priorities

As I reflect on what I have done well, and what I could have done differently in my life, the first area that comes to mind is work/life balance. Balancing my work and personal life with my family has not been a shining strength of mine.

When it comes to the way I spend my time, work has too often been the winner. Whenever anything came up at work that interfered with time spent with family, I felt obligated to fulfill my duties at work, above all else. Whether it was a trade show I needed to attend, a manufacturer visit, a customer visit, or an industry group meeting, I'd hop on a plane at the drop of a hat. When someone walked into my office with an important problem at 5:45 p.m. when I said I'd be home at 6:00, I'd finish the job no matter how long it took.

As if work weren't enough, my personal time was also a time-eater. Leading Horizon didn't end when I walked in the door at home, at least not as far as I was concerned. It was constantly on my mind, so whenever I could get some time alone to relax, read the newspaper, or do anything to get my mind off Horizon, I'd reach for it—often, at the expense of quality time with those I loved.

My involvement with Bible Study Fellowship (BSF) helped me keep things in perspective, but then again, that was two hours every Saturday morning and every Monday night away from home. Young Presidents Organization (YPO) also helped, yet those forums, too, took time. I went to conferences and retreats to learn more about business. I was on hospital, bank, and industry boards. I was committed to Fellowship of Christian Athletes, Pinnacle Forum, and served other local para-church ministries for students. I was a deacon at our church.

Yes, I was driven—driven by my desire to do it all and do it all with excellence. I understood the critical importance of my role in the family, but it was a constant challenge to perform well in all my capacities: as husband, father, leader at Horizon, and community volunteer.

When the girls were growing up, I justified my actions by thinking I was the CEO at work and Jeanene was the CEO at home. She graduated from the University of Illinois with a degree in Child Development, so she certainly knew what she was doing as a mother and teacher. She has good common sense, wisdom, and faith to go with that knowledge, so I knew that Jill, Carrie, and Marnie were in good hands. I trusted Jeanene unconditionally to lead the charge at home while I was away.

If you'd asked me at the time, I would have verbally acknowledged I believed that "family comes first." But, truthfully . . . my actions didn't show it.

Today, fathers are much more involved in the daily activities of home life. My sons-in-law put me to shame when it comes to quality time spent with their family. When the girls were young, Jeanene wasn't shy about letting me know she could use more of my help raising them. She had her hands full, and it seemed that whenever something broke around the house or one of the girls had a problem, I was out of town. I wanted to do more, but I couldn't let Horizon fail.

Finding Support

It remains hard for me today to understand how I *could* have put family first, while still meeting the responsibility I felt for the people of Horizon and all the others related to my personal endeavors. All I could do was recognize the problem and work at it. YPO in particular helped me make some much needed improvements.

Through YPO, I was given the unique opportunity to become friends with a group of entrepreneurs and leaders who were in very similar circumstances as my own. Our Illinois Chapter consisted of about fifty men and women who either owned companies or were CEOs in various industries. One of the best things about it was that our spouses were included in YPO programs.

I joined a member forum of ten men and women (mostly men) who met monthly to discuss business, personal, and family issues. Jeanene joined a spousal forum to discuss the same things, but from their perspective. Confidentiality and commitment were the primary requirements of the forum, which allowed us to share freely and get advice without any concern that it would be repeated elsewhere. We could say anything in this group and not be judged for it. It was so nice to be able to discuss matters I couldn't talk to anyone else about.

The confidentiality was maintained between couples as well. Jeanene didn't repeat what she knew about others in her group, and I didn't tell her what anyone in my group said, either. Highly personal issues were discussed in the forums, and serious damage to relationships and businesses could result if we shared information.

Balancing work and personal time around family was something all of us in my YPO forum were dealing with. By talking, and mostly listening, I learned the importance of:

- knowing our spouse's love language and observing it
- taking personality tests and using the results to grow in understanding of myself and my family members, and how we related to one another
- teaching our children independence and responsibility
- teaching them a healthy perspective about money and how to manage it
- quality time versus quantity of time with our children (they need both)
- knowing our children's schedules, so what they do becomes a part of our thinking
- the value of date nights to our marriage
- the need for time away from work

Some of these concepts were easy to put into practice, while others were hard work. However, knowing I wasn't the only one having the problem was helpful in itself, and hearing about the successes and failures of my peers was extremely valuable. Those discussions prepared me to think differently and at least be on alert for good ideas to better balance my life.

One day, Jeanene, being the wise woman that she is, asked if I could recite any of the girls' activities for the upcoming week. After I failed miserably, she said, "You have file drawers full of manila folders at the office for every manufacturer, every person you've talked with, every important letter written, all financial statements, para-church organization documents, and every other thing related to your work or personal life. How many folders do you have on our family?"

The answer, of course, was zero. Nada. None. I felt terrible.

So, I made four new file folders, one each for Jeanene, Jill, Carrie, and Marnie. Then I sat down with each of the girls and asked them to tell me in detail their schedule for the next week, along with why they liked or disliked each entry. I did the same for Jeanene, taking notes and putting them in my files.

It was such a small thing in the grand scheme of life, but just performing the act gave more depth to the way I thought about them when I was away. For example, Carrie was in middle school at the time—typically a difficult season for both parents and children. However, developing her folder helped me identify and appreciate her creativity and ability to communicate so well through the written word. It's been a joy to see those gifts blossom over the years into her success as a digital educator of home design, entrepreneur, blogger, and influencer.

We became intentional at making vacations special family times away from home—always limiting distractions as much as possible. It became tradition to jump in our conversion van and drive to Snowmass, Colorado or Sanibel Island, Florida a few times each year. This was before seatbelts (seriously!), and we had a bed-size section in the back, perfect for the girls to play games or sleep as we drove the 1,250 miles straight through. Before Horizon became successful, flying the whole family was out of our price range, but we didn't let that stop us.

We knew that getting away from home was necessary to unwind and devote quality time to our family.

We (Jeanene gets the credit) also became more intentional about having dinners together as a family. This is almost a forgotten art today, but we found it to be the one time every day when we were all together as a family.

A turning point for Jeanene and me as a couple occurred in the early '90s, when our friends Hazel and David Offner invited us to be part of their Community Bible Study (CBS) group. Hazel was the founder and leader of CBS locally. CBS is much like BSF except it was designed for mixed groups, a bit more casual, and a less intensive study. We enjoyed this enough that we both ended our long tenures as BSF discussion leaders and started our own CBS group.

Eventually, Hazel asked if we would consider taking on her role and become co-leaders of the city-wide program. In 1996, Jeanene and I began this task together. Hazel and Dave stayed involved to mentor us, and the two of them had an enormous impact on our lives. They taught Jeanene and me how to pray together, study together, and lead together. The key word is "together." It turned hours of individual personal time into hours with each other. This was a crucial step in the right direction.

A Family Affair

As the girls got older, we talked to them more about Horizon and what it meant to us. They all worked in the warehouse during summers and enjoyed getting to know the people there. It also taught them more about the company that had taken so much of Dad's attention over the years.

We began having family meetings to discuss the meaning of money, appropriate use of it, and the importance of generosity. As sons-in-law were added to the family, they too became part of the meetings, so they would be able to understand and work as a team with their wives. We tried to make Horizon a family affair.

I know my family had to feel like they came second, or even third, in my life much of the time because Horizon was always on my mind. Hundreds—if not thousands—of people depended on my leadership at Horizon—this was a pressing responsibility I couldn't just let go. It didn't feel like work for me, but a calling. And since Jeanene did such a great job at home, I didn't feel needed there as much as I did elsewhere. However, it pained me to think Jeanene and the girls felt like they played second fiddle.

That's why this strategic and intentional shift in priorities was so important to me. I wish it had been more natural for me to give my family the attention they deserved, regardless of the pull of other responsibilities, but I had to work at it. Every step I took—whether it was to call a family meeting to order, help orchestrate a family trip, or be there to talk with Jeanene and the girls about what was important to them—was purposeful, because I knew God was calling me to improve in this area of my life and my family deserved better than I was giving them.

Throughout my career, I felt God nudging me as He walked beside me. He was my inner companion with a full understanding of my life, my family's needs, and my own personal struggles. I believe He quietly put thoughts on my radar that would positively impact my family when I put them into action, just like when He prompted me to act in the business realm. I am no expert on being a great husband or father, but I am grateful for God's constant presence as I navigated the tension between my commitments.

I love my family. I also love others and feel responsible to fulfill my calling to serve both well. Perhaps there is always a healthy tension that sways back and forth between priorities, as we try to find the appropriate balance in every situation. I don't believe there is any easy, black-and-white answer for leaders who are navigating this tension. My biggest takeaway has simply been to follow God's lead, asking Him for guidance, and praying for my family as often as possible.

The Power and Priority of Prayer

In this current season of life, the one responsibility to my family that remains crucial for me is . . . to pray for them. I may not be involved in the day-to-day lives of my family (other than Jeanene), but I believe God knows all about them and is walking beside them as He has always walked beside me. He loves them and longs for their success in life.

Success in life has come to me as a direct result of acknowledging God's presence in everything around me and considering what His plan for me might be—during good times and bad. The same will be required of our children and grandchildren, of whom there are now eight.

And so, I pray every day for Jeanene, "That she will grow in her faith, and that she and I will grow together in faith, so that we'll have the same excitement about Jesus." I pray daily for our daughters and sons-in-law, "That each one will pray in their own way today, and take another step closer to God."

As each grandchild was born, I picked a character from Bible history that I believe he/she might grow up to be like, and used that disciple as a framework to pray for her/him. It's uncanny that just looking at a little baby would give me any indication of whom they might be like, but somehow their personality has always seemed to line up with the character chosen.

When the number of grandchildren reached eight, it took too long to recite all their names as I prayed for them, so I invented an acronym: SPELCHEK. This consists of the first letter of each grand-child's name starting with the youngest of the first four born (SPEL) followed by youngest to oldest of the second four (CHEK).

Steffen / Paige / Ellie / Lars   SPEL
Claire / Hans / Elizabeth (Liza) / Kate   CHEK

I thought it rather fitting that SPELCHEK is misspelled.

I pray every day for SPELCHEK, "That God will prepare them to accept Christ at an early age and that each will become a disciple of His." Individually, I pray that:

Lars *will become like a Peter—the one who ran after Jesus.* (Spontaneous, maybe not always thinking before acting, but devoted entirely without reservation to the Lord.)

Ellie *will become like a John—the one who loved Jesus.* (A kind, thinking person who understood Jesus more than most. A strong leader who inspired others to follow Christ.)

Paige *will become like a Philip—the one who couldn't help but tell others about Jesus.* (One who shared Jesus and His love boldly and with abandon, so others might not miss out on the greatest adventure in life.)

Steffen *will become like a James—the quiet, wise leader upon whom others depended.* (Jesus' brother, well respected for his wisdom and humility, working more behind the scenes maybe, sought out for counsel, a true man of God.)

Kate *will become like a Mary, mother of Jesus—the one who deeply believed God from the start and loved Jesus like no other.* (As a young girl, Mary immediately believed God when the angel told her His plan for her, and lived her entire life knowing Him so intimately in her heart.)

Liza will become like a Joseph—the one who had absolute faith in God, regardless of circumstances. (Even when bad things happened, Joseph trusted God's plan and confidently believed it would all be used for His glory, and it was.)

Hans will become like a Moses—the one who wasn't supposed to be here, but ended up leading His people out of bondage. (Hans was a surprise package who defied the odds by being born after his mother had a non-surgical sterilization procedure.)

Claire will become like a Queen Esther—the one placed where she was placed "for just such a time as this." (The only one in a position to save her people from extinction and did so at great personal risk to herself.)

What a blessing it is to be a grandfather! If history is correct, wisdom accompanies gray hair (which I have plenty of) and there is no one in the world I'd rather share wisdom with than our grandchildren.

At this time of my life, I understand better than ever the importance of family. I'm blessed to have Jeanene as my wife. And I couldn't be prouder of Jill, Carrie, Marnie and the men they chose to marry—Mike, Brad, and Joel. They are great fathers and mothers, husbands and wives, and faith is important to them all. Our eight grandchildren are growing up to be honorable and loving young people. It is a privilege to be part of their life. And it is a privilege to pray for them.

My good friend Roger always said, "Grandparents and grandchildren have a special bond, because we have a common enemy—their parents." This is a joke, of course, but we do enjoy showering love and wisdom directly on our eight grandchildren, as well as our prayers. And they enjoy our undivided attention (as well as getting almost everything they ask for).

Cousin overnights, family traditions that bring us all together, watching the children while parents are away, attending their sporting events, and "Cousins Camp" are some of the tools we use to love on our grandchildren. We can't get enough of it. The best is our annual Cousins Camp, when we take our grandkids aged five and over to Colorado for five days of fun with a purpose. We choose a camp "theme" (i.e., being a good friend, generosity, character, God's nature, persistence), have daily club times to discuss and relate the theme to real life, cook together, hike, ride horses, play games, and just have fun together. It's a special time to learn more about our grandchildren and share our lives with them.

The best times of life for me are still whenever I'm with Jeanene. But, it's a special treat to spend time with my sons-in-law and daughters and there is nothing so sweet and captivating as being with our eight grandchildren as they grow up. I am thankful to have more time today to enjoy them all.

14

Dream Big

Jeanene and I had seen some amazing things happen in our life that under ordinary circumstances would not have happened. But God is not ordinary. We loved the excitement and adventure of being involved in His miracles, so we tried to always keep Christ at the helm. Whether it was work, family, ministry, or community-related, we wanted every effort we entered into to serve God and be a good use of the resources He had entrusted to us. We wanted His dreams to become our dreams, and we wanted those dreams to be God-sized. God more than honored our desire.

One of the values we carried over the years had been a special place in our heart for those with disabilities, starting with a remarkable young woman named Marnie (not to be confused with our daughter of the same name).

Marnie Kottemann is the daughter of some college friends of ours. Shortly after her birth in 1983, she was diagnosed with Down syndrome. Marnie survived numerous illnesses over the years and grew up to be a beautiful young woman who lives independently with support from her mother. She made great friends through a local park district recreation program, Champaign Urbana Special Rec (CUSR).

In 2000, Marnie came to Snowmass, Colorado with her parents to attend our daughter Jill's wedding. A hike on the Ditch Trail was one of the planned activities that week. A favorite among locals for leisurely strolls, the trail follows an old irrigation ditch and is relatively flat with gentle grades and beautiful views of nearby Mt. Daly.

Marnie made it most of the way but when she got tired, Jeanene sat with her on a bench overlooking a beautiful valley while they waited for the rest of us to return. They had a delightful time sharing stories with one another, and the subject of weddings came up. Marnie said, "I'm going to get married on Flag Day, 2008!"

She obviously had thought about it and had the same hopes and dreams of any young girl of seventeen. As it turns out, she was only three months off her prediction. In March of 2008, Marnie married David, a young man who is an overcomer in his own right, like she is. The only reason it wasn't Flag Day was because she and David were both going to Disney World in April—a trip sponsored by CUSR—and they wanted to be married for that trip. It would be their honeymoon.

The wedding was beautiful as we watched these two innocent, lovely young people tie the knot. At the reception, Marnie, David, and about fifteen of their CUSR friends were sitting at a big, round table in the middle of the room. Surrounding them were a number of round tables of eight, filled with doctors, lawyers, business leaders, CUSR counselors, professors, and the like. Most of the toasts were given by those at the table of honor—Marnie and David's CUSR friends. The toasts were simple, heartfelt, and beautiful.

I looked around the room and paused as I took in the scene. I leaned over toward Jeanene and said, "Just look at this setting. This is how it will be in Heaven! The Bible says the last will be first and the first will be last. We're in the middle of a beautiful illustration of what that might look like."

Jesus pointed out many times that God loves everyone, and everyone is special in His eyes. Those who are poor, disenfranchised, or live with a disability—whoever may seem to be the "least of these" in man's eyes—will be given the table of honor in Heaven.[8] Those with power and influence will be on the sidelines. Marnie and David's wedding reception painted a picture we will never forget.

Larkin's Place

Three days after Marnie and David's wedding, we were scheduled to meet with a young mother and friend whose daughter, Larkin, had been born with Down syndrome. At that meeting, Amy asked us to consider helping her build a recreation center designed especially for people with disabilities in Champaign that she hoped to call Larkin's Place (LP). Having become a part of the community of local families affected by disability, she learned that when children with disabilities became adults they need "a place to go." At a young age, they are so cute that people accept them more freely. As adults, those with disabilities and their families often find themselves on the outside looking in, with no public place to go without being made to feel uncomfortable.

Jeanene and I had experienced this in a small way when we went places with our young friend Marnie as she was growing up. We had also learned more about it from attending a fundraiser for Challenge Aspen every August for the prior five years. The mission of Challenge Aspen is "making possibilities for people with disabilities." This organization brings people with disabilities and their families to Aspen and teaches them skills like downhill and cross-country skiing, whitewater rafting, horseback riding, swimming, gymnastics, hiking, and fishing. Challenge Aspen creates life-changing opportunities by encouraging participation in activities that redefine limits,

---

8. See Matthew 25:40

recognize abilities, and give newfound courage to everyday life for the whole family.

We felt it was no accident that Jeanene had had that special conversation with Marnie eight years prior; we had been drawn to Challenge, Aspen, and we had that awesome experience watching a grown-up Marnie get married. I can't help but think God had been working on this plan long before we had any hint of it! And, of course, the timing for Amy's ask was perfect. God is a master weaver and the threads in this tapestry were awe-inspiring.

We couldn't say no. At first, we thought we were being asked to write a check, which we were happy to do. However, she not only needed our money—she also wanted us to take a lead role in the project and help make it happen. After picking our jaws up off the floor, we decided there were just too many arrows pointing in this direction. This was something we needed to do.

Amy had been working on the project for two years and had come a long way. She brought us up to speed and we went to work with her. After tweaking the business plan, we began researching options. This rec facility needed to include a warm water therapy pool, and we soon learned that indoor water is *very expensive.* To do this right, we needed to partner with some other organization, preferably a financially sound one. Since we believed God was behind this, it was also important we had a partner that could freely acknowledge His principles.

The organization that seemed to align best with the Larkin's Place business plan was the local YMCA. The Y's mission is "to put Christian principles into practice through programs that build healthy spirit, mind, and body for all." It was founded on Christian principles, had a strong national brand, and is designed to be "for all." Unfortunately, our local YMCA was not in good shape financially, and was housed in an old mansion that was in very poor condition. It didn't pass the "sound financial footing" test. We moved on to talk with hospitals, park districts, colleges, and others.

When none of these seemed to fit the bill, we took another look at the Y. Even though they couldn't help financially, they seemed to be the perfect partner in every other way. I confided in my good friend and mentor, Tim Johnson, who surprised me when he said he used to lead a YMCA in Wichita. He loved the Y and encouraged me to pursue it. He also said he might have just the right guy to lead a new YMCA including Larkin's Place. Wow!

This was enough for Jeanene and me to believe God was leading in this direction for Larkin's Place. An outstanding group of ten Christian leaders agreed to either continue serving or join the board, a diverse group inspired to create a world-class YMCA for those with disabilities and those without. Tim agreed to be Chairman. It was October 1, 2008. (It's noteworthy that October 1, 1985 was the first day of operation for Horizon.)

Architectural plans were drawn for the new facility and we began the quiet phase to raise the money. It was to be a 75,000-square-foot facility with three pools, two gymnasiums, locker rooms, cardio and weight rooms, exercise studios, a child watch center, indoor playground, community rooms, offices, hospitality areas for people to come together, and a chapel.

This Y was also going to have sensory rooms, an elevator designed so those with disabilities could access the water slide, equipment that went beyond ADA requirements, soothing colors throughout to aid those with autism, and other features for families affected by disabilities. Larkin's Place was not to be a separate section of the Y, but a part of the whole. Larkin's Place would be woven into every inch of the building. Our plan was for those with and without disabilities to pass in the halls, mingle, become friends, and spend time together—all things critical to increasing understanding of those unlike ourselves.

We wanted everyone to feel comfortable, so our goal was to have a first-class feel without being fancy. We wanted it to be a landmark in the community and a stop on the tour for people considering a move to Champaign/Urbana. An attractive new Y with Larkin's Place (Y/LP) integrated into it could add to our community's micro-urban feel. We loved the design and drawings. We didn't love the price of eighteen million dollars to build.

God's Always in It

Everyone on the new board believed we had gotten this far because God was in it, but this was an enormous amount of money to raise in a community our size. If that weren't enough, we had just fallen into the worst recession since the Great Depression. Clearly, this was an impossible task . . . which really got me excited!

I could feel the adventure of watching God work coming on. Just like our survival after the Hobby Dynamics catastrophe. Just like the startup of Horizon. Just like the miracle of my landing at RP for my first job. Just like the van that was prayed for at Maranatha Bible Camp. This was going to be fun—I knew God would do it again.

We just didn't believe anything could be too big for God. We were advised to put the project on hold until after the recession, but we didn't think that was an issue if we were on the right track. In fact, it would just force us to rely on God more than ever. Any thought that we could do this because of our talent or connections was out the window. If this were going to happen, it would be by God's hand.

However, that didn't mean all we had to do was sit back and wait for God to do it. It would require work and prayer—lots of it. The board established a time to meet early in the morning once a week to acknowledge God's power and try to stay in alignment with His will. The next step was to find a great leader. *It always comes down to leadership!* Tim was a close friend of Coach Mark Johnson, the dean of Big Ten wrestling coaches. Mark had achieved outstanding success coaching at the U of I for the previous seventeen years. As it turned out, Coach had met his wife, Linda, at the YMCA, was inspired by Larkin's Place, and believed he could have a positive impact on more people as leader of the Y/LP.

Now that the pieces were falling into place, we began to ask for money. People with wealth have it because they were able to achieve an excellent return on investment in their business or career. When they consider charitable giving, they think exactly the same way—they expect an excellent ROI. Three things are necessary to show potential donors your project is worth their contribution: an inspiring vision, a solid business plan, and a great leader to execute the plan. We had all three.

Our strategy for the quiet phase of the campaign was to host small group dinners in our home to cast the vision and offer people an opportunity to become involved. We wanted these to be first-class events in order to show we knew what excellence looked like. The dinners were our first chance to indicate to potential investors we could build and operate a first-class Y/LP.

We presented the need in less than an hour near the end of the evening. The rest of the time we wanted to enjoy our guests, get to know them, and give them a relaxing and fun evening. The presentation consisted of Amy sharing her vision for LP, Tim, Jeanene, and I explaining our passion for the project, and Coach describing why this project grabbed his heart. As a former Olympian and winning coach, Mark had a powerful presence and made his determination clear to potential donors: "I don't lose!" Point made.

It was a solid team with God clearly in the lead. Matthew 25:40 was the central passage used to describe the higher purpose God had placed in our hearts for this project. "Truly I tell you, whatever you did for one of the least of these brothers and sisters of mine, you did for me."

Because God always shows up, about twenty very special people committed fourteen million dollars during this quiet phase of the campaign—enough to break ground on November 17, 2010. During the eighteen-month public phase of the campaign that followed, hundreds of families from the rest of the community caught the vision and provided the remainder. Total raised: eighteen million dollars.

The newspaper coverage the morning after ground breaking was by divine intervention. The lead picture was of our oldest grandchild, three-year-old Lars, laughing and playing atop a big sand pile on the property beside a six-year-old boy with Down syndrome. What a perfect image to display our goal with Larkin's Place—to build a facility in which everyone could play and recreate together, breaking down barriers that separate those with disabilities from those without.

One of the families who stepped up during the quiet phase of the campaign was my brother, Larry, and his wife Karen. This was not a project that would have caught their attention if Jeanene and I weren't involved. Yet, they believed that if we felt led by God to tackle this important project for the good of our community, they would do whatever we asked to help it succeed, just as they had done at Horizon.

The Y/LP was far from a simple project. Cost overruns could have been significant, but thanks to meticulous oversight by Coach and a high-quality contractor, the result was a beautiful building that serves as "a ray of hope in our community that inspires people to be better." It was miraculously finished on time and within budget. The building was completed in March of 2012.

Looking back, Jeanene and I marvel at what God did. We just "happened" to be close friends with Marnie and her family. We just "happened" to start attending Challenge Aspen events in 2003.

Jeanene just "happened" to be by Amy's side when Larkin was first born. The meeting scheduled with Amy just "happened" to fall a few days after Marnie and David's wedding (which Amy wasn't aware of). We just "happened" to be in a position to help. Tim Johnson just "happened" to be willing to help us lead the charge. Coach Mark Johnson just "happened" to have a soft spot in his heart for the YMCA. The Great Recession just "happened" to come along as we began fundraising to increase our need for dependence on God.

No, none of it "just happened." It all became part of a plan that was laid out long before any of us knew anything about it. God had a plan to help the "least of these" in our community and gave us the opportunity to join in His work. We took a giant step of faith forward, even though we couldn't see what was ahead. The result was an amazing accomplishment that some said couldn't be done—but God . . .

Keep on Dreaming

Another open door came into view after the Y/LP was completed when a neighbor gave us a call. Dr. Phyllis Wise had become Chancellor of the University of Illinois, Urbana-Champaign (UIUC) the year before and moved to a home just two houses from us. We had met Phyllis and her husband, but did not know them well. Phyllis asked if she could walk over for a short visit.

Over a glass of wine, she laid out her vision for a new Engineering-Based College of Medicine, one that would teach medical students engineering and medicine at the same time. Graduates would be prepared to think like engineers to solve everyday medical problems that physicians encounter. Combining the two disciplines would train the next generation of doctors to use technology and big data to invent solutions and processes to improve health care for people all over the world, at a lower cost. No medical school had ever trained physicians to be engineers in the same curriculum. It was a Big Hairy Audacious Goal (BHAG) that could change the way medicine is taught.

Jeanene and I jumped on board. We had seen what God can do with a good idea. He is Almighty God with limitless resources. When we see a BHAG that can help people physically, spiritually, and/or emotionally, our first thought is, *How can we make this work?* It's much easier to think about all the reasons something won't work and be quickly chased off. But, after all we'd been through, we had come to fear NOT dreaming big, more than the fear of failure. The potential problems of a venture must be thoughtfully considered but, if God is a part of it, we *know* it's possible. It's just a matter of finding a way to make it work.

There were plenty of reasons this idea wouldn't work. There had not been a new college added to the University for fifty years. The University of Illinois (U of I) system already had a big medical school in Chicago (UIC), though not engineering-based. The U of I trustees were almost all from Chicago and preferred growth to happen there over downstate. The State of Illinois was (is) essentially bankrupt and could not provide funds for this enormous undertaking.

On the other hand, our community was perfectly poised to take advantage of the possibilities! The UIUC College of Engineering was the only one in the Top Ten not connected to a College of Medicine. Our local downtown was poised to become a real micro-urban environment, attractive to the kind of talent the new COM would need. The U of I Research Park houses over one hundred twenty companies, many in the Fortune 500, and an incubator to assist researchers turn innovative ideas into startup companies. UIUC and the Carle Foundation Hospital System were the two largest local employers, but often operated in separate silos; this new COM would be a public/ private partnership that linked them together inextricably to create more powerful outcomes.

Dr. Wise believed success depended on a unified effort between the University, Carle, and the community. The unwavering support of all three was essential. This was the first time I had observed a U of I leader giving either the community or Carle equal ranking to the university. It was refreshing and genuine. Over the next two years, Jeanene and I spoke at community gatherings alongside Dr. Wise, Dr. Jim Leonard (Carle CEO), and other scientists and physicians to help cast the vision. Our role was to encourage the community to get behind the idea and provide the third leg of the stool alongside UIUC and Carle.

Progress was slow and the politics of a public undertaking like this one made Dr. Wise's job extremely difficult. We were not surprised. Any time one steps out of the pack with a BHAG, he or she can expect serious opposition from within and from without (just think of the biblical example of Nehemiah). But, Dr. Wise did an amazing job of staying on mission and not giving up.

But God . . .

> *"Nothing is more powerful than an idea whose time has come."*
> *(Victor Hugo.)*

Just when it looked like the project was headed for defeat and all seemed lost, a miracle occurred that saved the new COM. Remarkably, an unexpected change of governors led to a change in leadership for the U of I trustees. The new chairman was from downstate—a unique situation. With an open mind to the need for this new COM, the proposal for the first new college at the U of I for over fifty years easily passed.

An extraordinary group of deans and scientists at the U of I, along with Dr. Leonard and the Carle Foundation, carried Dr. Wise's vision forward, and the first class of thirty-two students arrived in the fall of 2018. Today over three thousand prospective students apply for the now forty-eight new slots each year. We played only a small part in this project, but answering the nudge to get involved gave us a front row seat for watching God work through an array of amazing people.

Jeanene and I aren't any more comfortable taking risks than the next person. But, any idea worth its salt has risk, and the bigger the dream, well, the bigger the risk. Failure can be extremely painful and public. Yet, every single time we have felt God's leading and taken that first terrifying step into the unknown, it has led to adventure and meaning far beyond what we would have experienced using our own logic.

Without knowing God and having a personal relationship with Him, without a spiritual life running in tandem with our physical life, we most certainly would have chosen safer routes. But oh, what excitement and joy we would have missed if our dreams had been limited to what we could see and understand.

15

Relationships

As I reflect back on what has impacted me most over the years, I am convinced that life is all about relationships. Throughout my life, it's been the people around me who have shaped me and given me joy. I believe we are wired to connect to God and other people from the time we're babies, and living abundantly depends on healthy, vibrant, and meaningful relationships.

I've been blessed by a number of special relationships and one of those has been my long friendship with Tim Johnson. Tim left the corporate world to start a local chapter of the Fellowship of Christian Athletes (FCA) in the early '90s. When he needed a spark to get it going, Jeanene and I were asked to help. I'd heard of FCA and loved the concept, but had never been involved personally. However, when I met Tim I saw his passion, and I was intrigued.

FCA was certainly in my wheelhouse. I love sports, especially basketball. I was never good enough to play organized sports, so I didn't have much direct contact with coaches. However, great coaches and star players were my heroes. Most everyone around me felt the same way. I recognized that coaches and athletes have a lot of influence and FCA is a ministry designed to help them use their platform to improve the lives of others through building a relationship with Jesus Christ.

Tim wanted to kick off this new local chapter with a "friend-raising" banquet, and he said he could get Tom Landry to be the speaker—if they had a sponsor with ten thousand dollars.

Now this really caught my attention. Tom Landry was a living legend! He was the first coach of the Dallas Cowboys, a position he held for twenty-nine years. He had retired only six years earlier, in 1988, so was still very much in the limelight. I figured if Tim Johnson could get Tom Landry for his first banquet, there was something special about this guy.

At that time, Horizon was just getting its first breath of air after the catastrophe of acquiring Hobby Dynamics, and profits were meager. But I felt connected to this mission. I felt like FCA had real potential to help others live a fuller, more robust life. If a great leader like Tim was going to be committed to it, I'd better get on board! It was a lot of money to us, but we said Horizon would sponsor the event.

Everything we had given up to that point had been anonymous and we wanted this to be as well, but Tim convinced us Horizon's reputation would give the idea credibility and encourage others to participate. So, we said yes to that, too.

FCA Illinois grew from that event to become a shining star in an FCA organization that is now in ninety-two countries, with two thousand staff members, over twenty thousand active huddles (small groups led by coaches or athletes), and reaching two hundred fifty thousand students at five hundred fields. Today, Tim leads the five-state Midwest Region and his work with FCA boards and staff members is used as a model in regions all over the world. He also is a play-by-play announcer and analyst for Big Ten and NCAA wrestling. His little dream grew into something huge.

Relational Investments

Tim didn't just take the money and run. He invested in me. We began meeting regularly to talk about what was going on in our lives, and pray for each other. When I struggled with depression, he was my go-to guy. When Horizon suffered a setback, I opened up to him. When he had an idea and wanted to try it out on someone, he came to me. If either of us learned something new, we'd take it to each other. We trusted each other.

There are few people in life you can trust with *anything*. If you have a handful of real friends whom you know will stand with you no matter what, you are a fortunate person. Tim is one of those people for me. We've encouraged each other, cried together, worked on projects together, prayed together, and challenged each other when we're wrong. He has mentored me and I him for almost three decades, and we wouldn't be the men we are today without our investment in each other.

Our friendship began with the advancement of FCA—and that's still on our front burner today. But, there is also more. We went on to push each other to build up other ministries, our community, non-profit boards, young leaders, a culture of generosity, and high-capacity leaders. Our desire to engage in the community and its leaders stems from our belief that biblical truths work just as well in secular organizations as they do in Christian organizations, and a community thrives when these truths are applied in both.

Tim is on a very special list of mentors who have come along in my life at the most opportune time to guide me toward the adventure, joy, and love that can only come from experiencing a spiritual life with God intertwined with a rewarding physical life.

Without any one of them filling the gap at just the right time, my story would be far less meaningful. Anyone who looks back can probably name a similar list of people who came into their life at just the right time, and greatly impacted who they are today. We make choices at every stage as to whether we listen to them or not.

I'm so glad I listened.

Effective Small Groups

In addition to one-on-one relationships, the "small groups" I've been involved in have had a sweeping influence on my life, going back to those early days when I started meeting with a few people to pray for Youth for Christ in our community. Because of these experiences and their lifelong impact, I've come to believe that *anything good that happens, happens through a small group.*

Some of these groups have been spiritually focused, but many have not. A company's Board of Directors, executive teams, teams of department leaders, task forces, committees, non-profit boards, city councils, production groups, school administrators, church leadership, Bible studies, forum groups—all are small groups of people that make big things happen.

Ideally, the perfect small group is between six and twelve people. Statistically, as the number dwindles below six, so do the differing viewpoints. As the number grows beyond twelve, there is less commitment and trust. The number of members dramatically affects the dynamic of the group culture and its effectiveness.

Great leaders know this and understand the magic that lies within these small groups of people. Generally, they apply it unquestionably in secular settings. Unfortunately, when it comes to faith (or anything personal), the relational emphasis that makes small groups so useful is sometimes viewed as a sign of weakness. Men, especially, seem to shy away from small groups beyond their career—possibly because they don't like the vulnerability. But, I have found intentional small groups to be much too valuable to ignore.

My very first small group in a personal or faith setting was the Bible study I did with the Navigators as a freshman in college. I knew nothing about the Bible, nor did I know the other guys in the group. It was intimidating to meet new people like this to talk about something I had no knowledge of. I was sure they all knew more than me (they did) and I'd certainly make a fool of myself (if I did, they covered for me). But, I went back weekly anyway, and I've welcomed the benefit of small groups ever since.

The most effective small groups are ones in which participants come prepared, as my first encounter demonstrated. We had a daily reading assignment and were asked to write down answers to questions that would spur thought and discussion. When we met, a facilitator loosely guided us through the study, but we talked mostly about how the topic of the week applied to our lives. There was no judging, everyone had a chance to talk, and good listening skills were practiced.

Later on, I realized how good this format is for any type of small group, faith-based or not. The success and meaning of that first Bible study drove me to make small groups a mainstay of my life. The list is extensive: Youth for Christ prayer group, Bible Study Fellowship, Horizon's Executive team, our Board of Directors, Young Presidents Organization Forums, Community Bible Study, Pinnacle Forums, YMCA/Larkins Place Board, University of Illinois College of Medicine Advisory Group, Carle Hospital Board, and the U of I Research Park Board of Managers. Work gets done in small groups. Lives are changed in small groups.

Two components are critical to an effective small group—confidentiality and commitment. **Confidentiality** makes it possible to throw out any wild idea or personal revelation that might be pertinent and helpful, without fear of it being judged or repeated outside the group. When confidentiality isn't assured, every thought is tempered by how it might be construed, misinterpreted, and judged out of context in another setting. Lack of confidentiality stifles discussion, often leaving the best ideas and most important thoughts unmentioned.

Commitment is critical, because if one person doesn't value the group enough to show up, it devalues the group for everyone else. One has to wonder how important the group is if others regularly call in with another excuse for missing. At the same time, the thoughts and ideas of the person missing are lost to the others in the group and vice versa. Of course, excused absences are unavoidable and accepted, but when one person's attendance is exceptionally low, it hurts the whole group.

Leadership Forums

Today, Pinnacle forums are the most valuable small groups with which I'm involved. Pinnacle Forum is a national organization that connects Christian leaders who want to achieve their God-given purpose. Through small group forums, leaders are encouraged and equipped to use their platform of influence appropriately to help others experience the joy and contentment that comes from acknowledging the presence of God.

Pinnacle forums follow the same format as YPO forums, in that they consist of individual updates on career, family, and personal matters along with member presentations. The only difference is the discussions are framed within the knowledge that God is involved in all those things happening around us. Some Pinnacle forums allow time for Bible study, but the meat of the meeting is designed to wrestle with the real issues that we all face in our career and life, but too often suppress.

For the past six years, I have facilitated a Pinnacle forum over Zoom, which has been especially valuable to me. It's a group of seven peers, each from a different industry and different city, from New York to Seattle. All of us were attracted to Pinnacle Forum, but traveled too often to attend local forum meetings regularly. So, we started meeting by phone and later by Zoom every two weeks. These are my go-to guys today who encourage and challenge me to live life to its fullest. I've never met some of these men in person, but the technology of Zoom has resulted in them becoming my best friends.

I also participate in a couples' forum and a CEO forum, both consisting of former YPO members. A few years ago, Tim Johnson and I led a group of middle-aged men who are leaders of their own forums to flesh out a greater understanding of God's purpose for them individually. One of our favorite ventures was leading what we called "Tomorrow's Leaders Forum"—a group of fifteen young, successful men with influence who wanted to hear how God has woven Himself throughout our lives.

One thing all these groups have in common—secular or faith-based—is they are peer-to-peer groups. I treasure relationships with people having far different lifestyles than my own. However, certain conversations involving work and personal trials can only be understood by others in similar situations—for example, when I was wrestling with the need to cut back personnel at work, banking relations, travel experiences, business acquisitions, selling a company, marriage issues, talking to our kids about wealth, or exploring our true purpose in life. Only people in a similar station in life can be understanding and helpful sounding boards for certain topics that are unique to your own demographic, interests, or calling.

As leaders, we are expected to always be in control and either have the answers or know how to find them quickly. Well, if we are honest with ourselves, we must admit we don't always have the answer, we aren't always in control, and we have doubts like everyone else! I used to believe that showing any kind of vulnerability to others would shatter their confidence in me and my ability to lead them. But, I came to understand that the strongest leaders are those with enough self-confidence to acknowledge their strengths and weaknesses and build a team around them with people able to perform far better than themselves in areas of weakness.

Showing vulnerability appropriately, and in the right settings, demonstrates strength, not weakness. We have to remember, people are smart! As a successful leader, I can put on a great show and even make myself believe I'm invincible, but the people around me know better. They know I'm not perfect. I'm only fooling myself if I think I can do it all on my own. Displaying vulnerability inspires loyalty and confidence in others like nothing else can. The safest place to do this is in small groups.

Mentors and members of my small groups have gone far in helping me become the best I can be. People who speak truth to my face—regardless of how uncomfortable it may be—have been invaluable to my becoming a better man. But, the true source of whatever success I have experienced comes through my personal relationship with God.

A Growing Relationship with God

To me, God is personal. He is a God who wants to have a relationship with me, a relationship that is personal and authentic, life-giving and intimate. He is just as real to me as Jeanene, or my friends on Zoom, or my forum guys, or Tim Johnson. Of course, God isn't visible, but that doesn't make Him any less real.

Over decades of spending time getting to know Him, I see God not only as the Creator of everything around me, but as a Father who loves me unconditionally. My children might disappoint me at times, but there's absolutely nothing they can do that will rock my love for them. God is that kind of Father . . . on steroids!

My spiritual life was a part of me from the moment I was born physically. However, I paid little attention to it until I was eighteen. Before that I felt in my gut that there was something more to life, but it didn't affect me in a physical sense, so I figured it wasn't worth my time to worry about. It first became real to me when those two guys from Campus Crusade explained what that feeling inside was all about. It was the One who created me, knocking on the door of my heart, and wanting me to open up to Him. Plugging into my spiritual life would unveil a whole new dimension of adventure and meaning. If I gave Him a try, He promised to give me an abundant life, today, and forever.

It was all so weird and uncertain back then. There was no way to prove any of this. Nothing about spiritual life can be proven by physical means. They are two totally different dimensions. So, the question for me then was, "Am I happy with my physical life alone? Or, could it be better by awakening my spiritual life?" I love adventure and want to be the best I can be, so I opened up to see what it was all about.

That was the *beginning* of my personal relationship with God— only the beginning. Developing a relationship with people requires spending time with them, and God is no different. This may sound odd to some, since God is not physical or visible. He is not accessible by our five senses. However, I believed there could be more for me and I dove into spending a lot of time with Him.

And, believe it or not, I got to know Him better. I did some reading in His Word, the Bible, to learn about Him. I talked to Him, as if He were there listening to me. I began to consider how the outcome of events in my life might actually be a result of what He promises to do in the lives of mankind. Maybe it wasn't a coincidence that what recently happened in my life occurred after talking to God about it. I felt like He had been in the background all along and now He was making Himself known to me.

As I learned more about Him, I started to realize how much He cares about me and wants a close relationship with me. One step toward Him from me, and He would carry me forward three steps. All it took was a little faith for Him to thrust me forward into a stronger relationship with Him and better life to live.

I began with a daily, five-minute "quiet time" with God. I followed the same format every time. I gave a minute or so each for praise, thanks, confession, and requests:

- **Praise:** for His love, mercy, almighty power, faithfulness, and other characteristics I'd learned about Him
- **Thanks:** for health, family, my job, a recent victory, or answered prayers
- **Confession:** for times I had ignored Him and lived life as if He didn't exist
- **Requests:** asking Him for help with a problem, direction, safety, health for my family, or relationships with people

It was pretty simple, but it was effective.

Reading, studying, and meditating on the Bible was time I set aside for Him to speak to me. I memorized some verses in the Bible that were especially meaningful to me. (Sometimes recalling and repeating these verses to myself brings His presence into focus during whatever I may be doing at the time.) I learned to listen to what He says in His Word and tried to apply it to my life. Sometimes I did this alone, but it was much better in a group where different thoughts and concepts about God could be heard and discussed openly.

Embracing friends who also have given God a chance has been a key part of my relationship with Him. Whether it's having lunch with someone, attending church, working on projects for the "least of these" with others, talking about business with them, or any activity of life—it's a good time to talk about how God is showing up.

Putting in the Work

Ayo Dosunmu is a great basketball player at the University of Illinois. He will be in the NBA for a long time. One thing I love about this young man is how he always talks about "putting in the work." He has a lot of talent, but he knows that if he wants to excel, he needs to put the work in—strength training, putting up thousands of shots, watching video over and over, practicing with teammates, studying the moves of NBA stars, talking to coaches, and working on his mental attitude. Michael Jordan, Kobe Bryant, Lebron James—they all had so much talent, but they are great because they worked at it constantly.

I mention this because of how well it illustrates the importance of effort and intentionality on our part. Few want to put the work in when it comes to building a relationship with God. But I knew that without it, I wouldn't go far. I didn't want to just play at it. If there was a spiritual life within me created by God, and He wanted to have a personal relationship with me, I was going to have to put in the work.

I gave everything I had to build my career and eventually Horizon Hobby. I took the same approach with my spiritual life as I did with my business career. I wanted to be the best at living life—both my physical life and my spiritual life.

I'll be the first to say that I'm not a "star" at this. I'm not great in so many ways, but I am great in God's eyes because I am who

He made me to be, as flawed as I am. I just keep moving forward and give it my best. I know I come up short, but that's okay. In the end, it's not the result that matters most. No, it's the effort we give, the journey, the process, and the course we choose every moment of every day.

That's what my life is all about: doing my best to stay on course, to live well physically and spiritually at the same time, and to surround myself with relationships that push me forward, edify, and build me up. That is how we experience abundant life—the best life. With others, and with God.

"I have come that they may have life, and have it to the full."
—Jesus (John 10:10b)

16

The Secret of My Success

Maybe I could have experienced the success I've had in business with or without recognizing God's presence in my life. But, activating my spiritual life has given far more meaning to the business success. I love doing deals, setting strategies for the future, uncovering opportunities within major disruptions, and growing companies. I get excited just thinking about it. However, leading people through those endeavors using biblical principles is what adds depth and meaning to it all. Biblical principles just work—it's as simple as that!

The three values we had at Horizon are biblical in nature: The Golden Rule, The Customer Is Boss, and the Inverted Pyramid org chart. Yet, it's hard to argue that they aren't some of the best concepts to use in running a business, whether you have faith in God or not. Putting your customers (others) first, treating every stakeholder in your company as you'd like to be treated, and leading strong from the bottom by providing people with all the resources they need to be successful constitute a pretty good formula for success. It certainly worked for us.

They also led to spiritual success. They defined my role as CEO, which was to promote, lead, guide, support, and, most of all, love those who reported to me, and teach them to do the same for their reports. Without saying it explicitly, we made Christ the bedrock of our business.

The result was an engaging, fun, and rewarding environment to come to every day for work. It was an environment that changed lives for the better by demonstrating how biblical principles work in business and are just as applicable in family and personal life. Not everyone bought in, of course, but those who did recognized the difference when they thought about it in spiritual terms. And, even if they didn't buy in, they still reaped the rewards of their leaders trying to do the right thing.

Two Worlds Collide

I've told the stories in this book to show that it is not only possible but uncommonly appealing to enjoy spiritual life right alongside our physical life. My physical life alone, the one seen by others, has been successful in terms of this world and I am very grateful. But that's just the outer shell. What people see is nothing compared to the success I've felt inside, in my spirit, as I've walked with God through every trial, tragedy, loss, mistake, and victory within my stories.

The unwavering goal of my life has been to live it to the fullest. I gave my all in every job I had to be unusually excellent, doing the best I could for the company and the people in it as if I owned it, whether I did or not. In the same manner, I wanted to be excellent in my role as husband, father, brother, and adult child to my parents. And my personal life with God was no different. I didn't want to "play" at living my spiritual life by giving it lip service, attending church and doing enough good deeds to make my scorecard with God look good. I wanted to give it my all.

In order to experience the richness and fullness of spiritual intimacy with God, I needed to live it in partnership with my physical life, not just put it in a "silo" that I visited on Sundays or when I was home, away from others. No, the true magic and wonder of success comes from a spiritual foundation that's made into an indispensable part of my career, family life, and every aspect of my personal life.

No silos. No compartmentalizing. No separating my job and faith, my family and faith, or my personal life and faith. Letting these worlds collide, by recognizing my spiritual life is just as real as my physical life and living with both of them in mind, is the reason for my success in business and in life.

I've found that the Spirit of God is always working deep within me and that, when I pay attention to Him, I get a taste of an abundant life. *My definition of Abundant Life is when I'm in alignment with my Creator.* When I feel close to Him. When I see His Hand all over what is happening in my physical life. When I feel like I'm on target with Him. This gives me contentment, joy, peace, and an attitude of gratitude. It's when I feel comfort deep in my heart when the world would say I should be worried sick. It's when I'm almost able to see the face of God.

God wants us to live an abundant life. I believe it's the life we'll experience in Heaven when we're with God, because then we'll be in tune with Him all the time. *But, abundant life isn't just for Heaven.* God intends for us to live it right now, right here on Earth, and gives us all we need to do it. It comes when we take our spiritual life off the back burner and acknowledge God's presence in the things we do.

As I've studied and applied what the Bible says about life, I've found it to add another dimension that frames my finite physical life within an infinite bigger picture. I've come to believe physical life by itself is two-dimensional. When we open the gift of spiritual life with God, a third dimension emerges and everything becomes more vivid and more real. A life that was limited to what man can discover and learn becomes full and limitless as we begin to experience the world of our Creator.

At first glance, living in alignment with God may seem unattainable, but if I can experience it, anyone can. The beauty of God's design is that it's the journey that matters, not the end result. He knows we're not perfect and doesn't expect us to be. Life gets good simply because we begin to acknowledge and respond to His presence around us, and over time learn to do it more and more.

One Source of Truth?

Here's a story I lived personally a few years ago that illustrates my thinking about God's truth versus what mankind believes to be true.

I was sitting in my car, stopped for a red light at a busy intersection. There was a car turning left in front of me, sitting in the middle of the intersection, waiting for oncoming traffic to pass. He apparently thought the coast was clear because he made the turn, but there was an oncoming car he didn't see, going about twenty miles an hour. There was an awful sound of crunching metal. We all got out of our cars and ran over to help. Fortunately, everyone was all right, though severely shaken.

The police arrived and began taking accounts of what happened. I explained that the man turning left obviously didn't see the oncoming car and turned in front of it on a green light. Open and shut, right? Not quite.

The guy sitting in the car next to me said the light had just turned and the oncoming car was at fault for running a red light. What? How could that be? Our light was red, even after the accident. A lady walking on the sidewalk nearby said the oncoming car was going fast, probably fifty miles an hour, so it was her fault for speeding. The two people involved in the accident also had their own (different) versions of what happened.

These were all *eye-witness accounts*. Every one of us could say, "I was there. I saw it clearly and this is what happened." So, why wasn't there a single story that relayed the actual truth?

A friend of mine often says, "There is *your* truth, and then there is *my* truth." Are there really two or more truths to every situation, argument, political discussion, or car accident? Is truth relative? Can it be different based on our upbringing, social interactions, choice of friends, education, experiences? I don't think so. There can be different perspectives, but there's only one truth.

There is one true account of what happened in that car accident. However, we'll never know the real truth because every witness came to the scene with a different set of biases. The guy in the car next to me might have glanced at his phone while waiting at the light and missed the impact, innocently making up what he thought he saw, based on past experiences. The lady on the sidewalk saw the oncoming car from the side, so it looked to her like it was going faster than it really was. Maybe the light really had changed, and my own account was wrong.

This scenario plays out in many areas of our lives. "Truth" can appear to change for us because we have a limited view of what's before us. For centuries, the world was flat. Scientists everywhere confirmed it was true! Until . . . they learned it wasn't. Scientists have theorized about the number of galaxies that exist, how old the earth is, what dinosaurs looked like, or how the shape and size of the brain can predict mental traits. Their theories were all true, until they weren't anymore.

Truth is defined as "a fact or belief that is accepted as true" (Webster). Though we are always striving to find the truth, mankind's view is severely limited. What we believe to be true today based on all available knowledge, we often find out later isn't true based upon further study and discoveries.

However, there is one truth about all things that supersedes man's knowledge. Truth doesn't change. So, who could be the arbitrator of truth other than our Creator, who is never changing? If history has shown us what man "accepts as true" keeps changing with new discoveries every day, then the only truth known in the physical realm is pretty slippery.

I've been a nature lover from my earliest years. I remember lying in the grass in our front yard when I was seven, looking up and watching the clouds change shape in the sky as they passed by, or the leaves swaying in the wind, feeling the green grass under my fingertips or the warmth of the sun so far away. I remember considering the air I took into my lungs and how my body worked in such mystifying ways for me to be able to breathe and move the way I could. How did all this come to be?

I've heard Ken Blanchard (author of *One-Minute Manager* and *Lead Like Jesus*) challenge his audiences by saying, "Let's assume you're a really smart person. In fact, you are the smartest person in the world! You may know more than anyone else has ever known, yet with all that knowledge, you still wouldn't know even one percent of what there is to know in the world." His point is that man's knowledge is finite, bound by what has been learned and experienced by humans on Earth.

The Word of God is where the spiritual realm meets the physical realm. Reading the Bible was, for me, so intimidating and implausible at first, but it was the only place to go to learn about truth beyond man's understanding. The more I tested the Word of God (the history of mankind and promises of God), the more I experienced His presence and guidance in my life. For over fifty years, I have tested and proven out His Word. I am still a babe in the woods when it comes to the knowledge of God and His infinite being, but that's part of the reason it's so exciting. There is always so much more to learn.

Experiencing God

In Henry Blackaby's book, *Experiencing God*, he describes Seven Realities for experiencing God in extraordinary ways. It resonates clearly for me as I've watched God work in my life. The Seven Realities identify how God has been involved in my physical life. They are:

- God is always at work around you.
- God pursues a continuing love relationship with you that is real and personal.
- God invites you to become involved with Him in His work.
- God speaks by the Holy Spirit through the Bible, prayer, circumstances, and the Church to reveal Himself, His purposes, and His ways.
- God's invitation for you to work with Him always leads you to a crisis of belief that requires faith and action.
- You must make major adjustments in your life to join God in what He is doing.
- You come to know God by experience as you obey Him, and He accomplishes His work through you.

All my stories can be related to every single reality described above. A few dramatic ones are my decision to give God a chance at NIU, accepting my first job, asking Jeanene to marry me, starting Horizon, buying Hobby Dynamics, turning Horizon into a 100% ESOP, leading the drive to build the YMCA/Larkin's Place, and selling Horizon to private equity. Framing such decisions within the Seven Realities describes the ongoing experience of living my spiritual life in tandem with my physical life. You may be able to do the same based on your own life stories.

My physical life is strong and I'm going to squeeze every drop out of it I can. But, it remains *finite*, and everything I accumulate and enjoy in this physical life will come to an end. My spiritual life, on the other hand, is *infinite*. It adds greater depth to every experience of physical life. Why would I ever be satisfied living my life within physical limits when it offers only a fraction of the possibilities?

The truth is, making faith the bedrock of my career has led to greater success than I would have ever imagined—in business, with my family, and at play. I see so many high-capacity leaders settle for less than what life has to offer because they think they have it all figured out. They lock their eyes on financial success, power, influence, fame, family, or something else from this physical life and they may do it really well. All the while, they are missing the entire spiritual dimension of life.

I've always loved riding Harleys across the country, and snowboarding in two feet of fresh Colorado snow. These two things have something in common, and it's this: where you lock your eyes is where you'll go. If you are negotiating a turn on a Harley, you do not want to look down! You need to lock your eyes on the road as it turns in the distance, and you'll automatically go there. On a board, if you want to turn to the right, you have to bend your neck around and lock your eyes to the trees on that side. It's amazing how your board will start turning that way on its own.

I decided to give God a chance over fifty years ago, and learned I needed to lock my eyes upon His truth if I wanted to live life to the fullest. It has not been without disruptions and detours, but striving to live the best life I can with God in this physical world has been a journey well worth living. My eyes are still locked on Him, and I look forward to what He has for me next.

What Does It Mean For You?

I guess the question then becomes: what are your eyes locked on? Are you living your physical life to the fullest, squeezing every single drop out of it you can, and settling for its rewards? Striving only for things this world has to offer provides fleeting success at best. My contention is that to get the most out of life you cannot leave your spiritual life on the shelf, gathering dust, to be pulled out only occasionally. Framing everything we do in this limited physical world, *within the limitless world of God,* is the only way I know to experience life at its fullest.

I hope that my story encourages you, because engaging the spiritual life God has created within you will not only take your life to new dimensions, it will make the lives of all those you lead more pleasant, fulfilling, joyful, and rewarding.

The gift of a spiritual life with God is right there for you. Accepting the gift, putting in the work, and applying Christ's truth to all aspects of your life make up the true blueprint for success. It doesn't necessarily mean financial success, or the ideal marriage, or perfect health, although those areas of your life will certainly be impacted. I'm talking about the joy and fulfillment that come from an integrated physical and spiritual life, lived in relationship with God and alignment with His Word.

God is right there, in plain sight, waiting to offer you the fullest, most abundant life you can imagine!

STUDY GUIDE

Introduction

Christian business men and women, as well as many other professionals, often struggle to find spiritual purpose and meaning in their work. So many Christian professionals live two lives: one at work and one in their faith community. This study was written in part to help you bring the two halves together, and inspire you to experience greater joy and success in your work and life as you embrace the spiritual life God has given you in tandem with your physical life.

Before working with Rick on this study, I had heard him speak countless times. He is in demand from the sort of groups and organizations that value excellence in leadership, business success, and how a faith commitment impacts one's life—oftentimes all three topics wrapped in one speech. His life story is an interesting one, and at times he seems to be as surprised as anyone at the success he has experienced. It is this sort of humility that endears him to many different kinds of people.

Rick's favorite life verse is woven throughout his story. "'For I know the plans I have for you,' declares the Lord, 'plans to prosper you and not to harm you, plans to give you hope and a future.'" (Jeremiah 29:11) One of the keys to his seemingly unshakeable confidence is his belief that God is in control. He firmly believes that God is writing the story of life, and inviting all of us to join His story and perhaps help write a line or two. It is this unbending confidence in God's plan that makes Rick's life worthy of study.

For Rick, *In Plane Sight* is not his story as much as it's God's story. "I couldn't have written that script, but I think God could—and He did!" Our hope is that this study will help you discover that same confidence, and find your own story within God's story.

—Joe Thomas
Professor of History of Christianity,
Urbana Theological Seminary
Founder and President, Life Together House

Chapter 1: Foundations

Chapter Synopsis

After the tragic loss of his high school sweetheart, Rick entered college with a lack of direction. When he was still struggling with his grief, grappling with the meaning of life, and feeling a deep sense of loneliness, two campus ministry groups shared the gospel with Rick and deepened his Christian faith through discipleship. When he transferred to the University of Illinois to study business, Rick was swept up in the late 1960s counter-cultural, anti-establishment rhetoric. His new companion, Jeanene Flowers, helped him wrestle with his faith questions as he put God on hold for three years. With time, Rick discovered that God continued to walk beside him, even during this time of questioning. With a nudge from the Holy Spirit, he returned to Bible study and prayer. Simultaneously, he received good news about a job opportunity in Champaign.

Key Bible Verses

Two young men from Campus Crusade for Christ (CRU) shared *The Four Spiritual Laws* with Rick. Take time to read and meditate on these four verses that form the starting point for establishing a personal faith in Christ.

John 3:16

For God so loved the world that he gave his one and only Son, that whoever believes in him shall not perish but have eternal life.

Romans 3:23

For all have sinned and fall short of the glory of God.

Romans 6:23

For the wages of sin is death, but the gift of God is eternal life in Christ Jesus our Lord.

Revelation 3:20

Here I am! I stand at the door and knock. If anyone hears my voice and opens the door, I will come in and eat with that person, and they with me.

Discussion Questions

1. Rick experienced a time of deep pain and suffering with the death of his girlfriend, Nelda, when he was seventeen. There is a profound mystery about how God uses our suffering to further His purposes. What are your thoughts on this? Have you experienced this in your life or seen it in the life of someone you know?

2. Rick wrote, "God wanted to have a personal relationship with me, one in which He would love me and I would love Him. It wasn't about keeping score of good and bad things done; it was about trust in Him as my Creator, my Father, and my Friend." How do you keep yourself focused on building a personal relationship with God instead of keeping a "scorecard"?

3. Rick spent the first two years of his Christian life being discipled one-on-one, meeting in Bible studies, and attending summer conferences. He learned how to spend time with God and came to know Him personally through His Word. These early activities created a spiritual foundation for the rest of Rick's life. Is this something you were taught as a new Christian? What does your time with God look like today?

4. His good friend, Dave Larsen, provided a priceless gift to Rick when he confronted him about his future, saying, "Rick, I know you are going to be successful in life! The question is . . . will you be successful in the world's eyes, or in God's eyes?" This was a tough question. If you reach your goals and are successful, what will your life look like in five years?

5. Rick wrote about the Holy Spirit showing up in his life. (p. 19) What role have you seen the Holy Spirit play in your life?

Rick's Life Lessons

"Somehow for the first time I felt that I not only had a physical life on Earth to live, but a spiritual life that ran parallel and it would live forever." (p. 9)

"He touches my life every moment of every day to show His love and encourage me to live in a way that gives me the most joy, peace, and love I can possibly experience. That's all He wants. And everything He does in and around me is designed to help me get there." (p. 11)

"Once one starts down this road of mistrust, there is no end to it." (p. 15)

"This might have seemed to be an inconsequential stop along my journey, but God doesn't waste any of our time on Earth." (p. 18)

"Expecting others to make decisions based on my assumptions is a fool's game. Like never before, at Goldblatt's I learned to respect every person regardless of color, status, beliefs, or anything else. This foundational truth became very important to the success I would experience later in life." (p. 18)

"As I wrestled with this, I believe the Holy Spirit showed up." (p. 19)

Chapter 2: Priorities

Chapter Synopsis

Rick landed a new job opportunity at Research Press. Within two weeks, he was named Operations Manager, and he grew in confidence as he recognized his gift for business and leadership. He was named president and began to oversee the expansion and profitability of the business for almost five years. His vision for the future of Research Press eventually began to clash with the owner. Sensing from God that it was time to move on, Rick nevertheless decided to stay put, choosing security over faith. But, God will not be denied—uncomfortable with Rick's vision for the future of the company, the owner eventually fired Rick. Two weeks later, he landed a new job with Great Planes Model Distributors.

Rick and Jeanene Flowers were married in 1972. Jeanene's role as Rick's partner grew as she offered support and timely advice for his career. They had three daughters together. Rick's spiritual growth continued as he found mentors who taught him how to stay close to God. His great respect for para-church organizations, such as Youth for Christ and Bible Study Fellowship, continued to grow as he recognized how they complement the work of the church.

Key Bible Verse

Isaiah 55: 8-9

"For my thoughts are not your thoughts, neither are your ways my ways,"
declares the Lord.

"As the heavens are higher than the earth, so are my ways higher than your
ways and my thoughts than your thoughts."

Discussion Questions

1. Rick specifically prayed for God to help him meet more mature Christian men who could mentor him in faith. God answered his prayers with David Gardner and Bill Edwards. Whom would you consider to be your mentor(s) in the Christian faith? How have they modelled the Christian faith? Are you in a position today to mentor someone in his or her faith?

2. One of the things Rick really respected about Bill was how he did not hide his faith for the sake of business. "In my experience, successful people tended to hide their faith, not wanting to offend a potential client or customer. It was okay to believe in God, but faith had its place and it wasn't in business. But Bill didn't subscribe to this theory. God was a part of everything he did, and he let everyone know it." (p. 24) What are your thoughts on how faith and business/career connect?

3. One thing we saw repeatedly in Rick's story is how God planted seeds that did not sprout until years later. Rick wrote, "Through the books we published, Jeanene and I were given a heart for those with disabilities. This passion was instrumental in decisions we made later." (p. 27) What do you take from this reflection?

4. Rick mentions several times in his life story about getting "a gut feeling" about things, and he believes these gut feelings are from God. How does God communicate with you? How do you distinguish between a feeling in your gut and a communication from God about a specific situation? (especially as it relates to your business or career)

5. Jeanene plays a vital role in Rick's life and career. She provides him emotional support when he needs it and kicks him in the butt when he needs that, too. Do you have someone who plays this role

in your life? What are your greatest needs that only someone else can fulfill?

Rick's Life Lessons

"This is when I first learned that responsibility is not so much given as it is earned." (p. 21)

"I remember spotting this businessman secretly giving [the leader of Youth for Christ] hundred-dollar bills on the side. Giving that much money away, freely and without fanfare, caught my attention." (p. 23)

"Communication solves so many problems. My natural tendency was always to shy away from conflict, but whenever I met it head-on, all the wrong assumptions made on both sides could be discussed and cleared up. Without communication, the wrong assumptions just multiply." (p. 26)

"I soon learned that not following God's lead carries far greater risk than taking a step into the unknown with Him." (p. 28)

"But fear of the unknown locked me in place, and I waited until I was forced out." (p. 29)

". . . but, as usual, God had something in mind. He was just waiting until I left RP (Research Press). Since I didn't have the courage, He made the decision for me." (p. 31)

Chapter 3: Leading from Behind

Chapter Synopsis

Rick began work at Great Planes. No longer president, he faced the humbling task of being "nothing more than an assistant to the president." As in his previous job at Research Press, he quickly identified ways in which to improve the efficiency and profits at Great Planes. The owner's trust in Rick increased as he recognized Rick's contribution to the company. Still, Rick never felt completely at ease at Great Planes, even as he worked hard to position himself to advance up the ladder of leadership and responsibility. Rick embraced the approach of intrapreneurship. He sensed that God had something more in store for him.

Rick's time at Great Planes allowed him to grow his business acumen. Faced with difficult business challenges, he learned how to engage his team and create strategies that proved effective. In an industry where suspicion ran high against the company he worked for, he built trust with store owners and established great customer service. Finally, he observed how a real entrepreneur calculated the true worth of companies, which helped him learn the ropes of buying businesses in the future.

Rick's faith continued to mature, especially as it pertained to the ups and downs of business. Learning to distinguish between his own voice and God's voice proved difficult. Still, his trust in God to take care of him and his family grew over time as he saw God at work. Rick's belief that God had a greater adventure in mind for his life only solidified throughout these years—so much so that when he was fired for a second time in five years, he did not panic, but looked forward to the future with confidence.

Key Bible Verse

Colossians 3:23

Whatever you do, work at it with all your heart, as working for the Lord, not for human masters.

Discussion Questions

1. The concept of "intrapreneurship" was something Rick embraced. How was this helpful for him during his years at GP? How did it shape him as a recruiter for leaders later in his career? What do you think about this concept and your company?

2. On page 38, Rick describes a difficult business challenge that confronted him and his team. Describe a business problem you have faced in your work and how you overcame it. What do you think of Rick's approach to overcoming his challenge?

3. Rick had a courtside seat to several personality conflicts during these early business years. What can we learn about dealing with people from Rick's observations and actions?

4. In 1984, Clint Atkins entered the hobby business. He was an astute businessman and fierce competitor. Have you tangled with a fierce competitor like Clint Atkins? What positives and negatives came out of that competition? How did they change you as a businessperson?

5. Rick was sorely disappointed when he was fired instead of being promoted to President of Hobbico. By his own admission, he

missed what God was up to in his life. He was hearing his own voice instead of God's. What can we learn from this episode in Rick's life?

Rick's Life Lessons

"Like at Research Press before, I persistently pushed to gain more authority and it paid off for me and the company. I remember more than once telling Don, 'I want the job you're doing, so you can do new things no one has time for now that will take the company to a new level.'" (p. 37)

"My career was headed for a jolt. I thought, *I don't know what God has planned for me in this, but He is in control and it will be okay.* This attitude gave me a sense of peace that turned what could have been a very stressful situation into an interesting adventure." (p. 40)

"He did this to create the perfect job for me. It sure seemed like this was God's plan. But . . . I was wrong. I didn't realize it then, but God was actually preparing me for something much bigger and better." (p. 41)

"This is one of the many incidents through which Jeanene and I learned to look for the big picture in all aspects of our life, including when facing disappointment and failure . . . God had shown us that He was in control. In our kitchen that night, we had a strange sense of anticipation that this time, we were on the cusp of something really big." (p. 43)

Chapter 4: The Promised Land

Chapter Synopsis

Rick decided to start a business of his own. After two firings in five years, Jeanene joked, "Rick needs a company of his own because it may be the only way he can ever hold a job!" God directed Rick to the story of Abraham—specifically, Abraham's trust in God when he was called to leave his comfortable life and move to a foreign land, the Promised Land. Rick had a hard choice in front of him: take a new job offer, which would have provided a steady paycheck and more money, or follow God's lead and start a new business with many unknowns. As the pieces fell into place, he perceived that God was confirming his decision to start a business.

But when pressure mounted on a friendly local bank president and the expected financing disappeared, Rick plunged into despair. Over a long and distressing weekend, God reaffirmed to Rick and Jeanene that He wanted them to move forward by reminding them of Abraham's journey. The next week, Rick found another bank to offer the needed line of credit, but it was contingent upon raising $150,000 in committed equity.

Rick forged ahead with the necessary preparations to ship product by October 1st. He proceeded to lease a building, hire staff, buy equipment, order product, and began taking orders from customers. The pressure continued to build! He beat the pavement and knocked on every door to raise the equity, to no avail. Finally, at a Sunday lunch at his parents' house, his father and brother agreed to put up the necessary equity, along with Rick's contribution, to satisfy the bank. Horizon Hobby was born! The Promised Land was in sight.

Key Bible Verse

Genesis 12: 1-5

The LORD said to Abram, "Go from your country, your people and your father's household to the land I will show you. I will make you into a great nation, and I will bless you; I will make your name great, and you will be a blessing. I will bless those who bless you, and whoever curses you I will curse; and all peoples on earth will be blessed through you." So Abram went, as the LORD had told him; and Lot went with him. Abram was seventy-five years old when he set out from Harran. He took his wife Sarai, his nephew Lot, all the possessions they had accumulated and the people they had acquired in Harran, and they set out for the land of Canaan, and they arrived there.

Discussion Questions

1. A significant part of Rick's story is the self-realization that he was to have his own business. How does one know if he or she is to be an owner? What insight gathered from Rick's life can help you answer that question?

2. Rick had the opportunity to accept a secure job that paid more money than he made at GP. This had to be tempting, with only two to three months of financial reserves to live on. Rick refers to this as "the safe option." Have you ever been tempted to take "the safe option" instead of what looked like God's option for your life? How did you know the difference? What did you do?

3. At the end of his time at GP, Rick misread God's intentions for his future and believed that he was going to be the new President of Hobbico. Upon leaving GP, he was equally sure that God wanted him to start a new business. Does Rick's story give us any clues on how God speaks to us, how we are to interpret it, and what actions we are to take? What role did Scripture play?

4. Rick was determined to maintain control of his own company, even as he desperately needed equity to get it going. He dug in his heels on this principle: "So I could set my own vision and lead Horizon the way I wanted." How important is it for the founder to have a clear vision for his or her company?

5. Rick referred to the financial commitment his father and brother made to the company as "a once-in-a-lifetime experience." That is a powerful statement. In your business or field of work, have you experienced any once-in-a-lifetime experiences? If we follow God into a foreign land, should we expect a once-in-a-lifetime experience?

Rick's Life Lessons

"Jeanene and I never lived beyond our means but in our younger stages of life, we struggled to build emergency funds. It's hard to save money when you have a young family and are still building a career. We knew we didn't have much time, but we decided to use what time we had to look for a way to get into my *own* business." (p. 45)

"Jeanene and I kept asking God to show us what He had in mind. His answer seemed to be, 'Start a hobby company like GP. Yes, it's dangerous but I am with you; you can do all things through me.'" (Philippians 4:13) (p. 47)

"I knew we were attempting an impossible task. The only way it would work was if God's hand was on it. But, history told me, that's the way God likes it. When faced with an impossible task like this, life becomes *real and raw*. Our eyes become wide open. We're alert and we make every moment count. And we have no choice but to rely on God." (p. 49)

"Immediately, Larry and Dad both responded nonchalantly, 'Let us help, then. We always thought this was the right way to go, anyway. Maybe now you'll let us finally help you.' They acted like it was no big deal. They carried on like this is just what family does. I told them my plan of $37,500 from each of them and they said, 'Let's do it. Don't worry about it; we'll be fine.'" (p. 55)

"I didn't jump for joy, or yell, or even get excited. It was a sobering moment because of the immense responsibility I felt. However, the moment also confirmed to Jeanene and me that Horizon was a Promised Land given to us by God. **Horizon was bigger than us.** It was God's company and He was in charge of every detail. He was trusting me to lead it." (p. 55)

Chapter 5: Miracles

Chapter Synopsis

Seeking to establish a God-directed company run on God-ordained principles, Rick related the early days of the electrifying start to Horizon when "everyone was equal" and the "team was one body." Horizon met its October 1st start date of shipping product to customers, but only because of the perseverance of the whole team. Within three months, they reached the low end of the entire first year's projection. By the end of the first year, they achieved their high-end goal.

Jeanene gave Rick more than one pep talk to keep him going. At one point, early in the process, she even predicted the company would reach its highest financial projection! It did, and it cost Rick a mink coat, which was well-deserved as a reward for all Jeanene's hard labor as Rick's "personal coach." By the end of the first year, Horizon opened a West Coast distribution center and Rick's brother, Larry, became its leader. Horizon Hobby was not only serving a higher purpose, but continued to be a family affair.

Key Bible Verses

Matthew 7:12

So in everything, do to others what you would have them do to you, for this sums up the Law and the Prophets.

Matthew 23:11

The greatest among you will be your servant.

Discussion Questions

1. Rick gave a lot of thought to the "DNA" of his business because he believed there was a correct way to ensure the vision, mission and values of Horizon Hobby. Think about the DNA of your business or organization. What is it? How difficult would it be to reset it?

2. How did Rick go about setting his vision, mission, and values for Horizon? How did he incorporate them into the organization? What do you do to ensure the vision, mission and values of your organization are not only clear but followed?

3. At various points during the process of starting Horizon, Rick had key people help him push through his doubts and persevere. Dietrich Bonhoeffer spoke about the gift one Christian can give to another as they live life together: "The Christ in his own heart is weaker than the Christ in the word of his brother; his own heart is uncertain, his brother's is sure." What people are in your life to speak words of encouragement to you? Who helps you persevere when you are ready to give up?

4. What strengths and weaknesses are associated with having family members involved in your company as financial partners and co-workers? How does Rick negotiate these matters?

5. Do you have something like the "20 Basics" to help everyone understand how they are expected to do their jobs? Which three of Horizon's "20 Basics" are your favorite? Why?

Rick's Life Lessons

"Many persons have a wrong idea of what constitutes true happiness. It is not attained through self-gratification but through fidelity to a worthy purpose." Helen Keller

"Orders kept coming and we shipped every single one the same day it came in. If it meant working late or bringing everyone from the office to the warehouse to pack orders, we did it. We gave the warehouse people little thank-you cards they could sign and stick in each order. I wrote a personal note on every invoice mailed for several months, just to let customers know how much we appreciated them. We were all tired, but the adrenaline kept pumping. It was exciting, fun, and incredibly rewarding." (p. 59)

"I believed this was another example of God showing up, after I'd done everything I could do, proving that He's always with me and will bring forth His plans when I'm ready to listen. It's often when I get to the end of my rope that something really good happens." (p. 63)

"Jeanene and I started Horizon because we believed a business could be the most fun, meaningful, efficient, and profitable when it is run with God's principles at the center. We were convinced an environment based on biblical values was not only better for people, but it was also a recipe for a better business. So far, that was proving to be true. It certainly felt like God was involved every step of the way." (p. 64)

"What if work was a place that inspired people to love each other and treat everyone like we would like to be treated? All kinds of good things would come from that. Strong, caring relationships would be built with customers, manufacturers, suppliers, and everyone our people came into contact with. Service levels would be excellent. And the same attitude would bleed over into employee's personal lives, making them better spouses, parents, friends, and citizens." (p. 65)

Chapter 6: When Disaster Strikes

Chapter Synopsis

Five years into a remarkable start to Horizon Hobby, Rick was faced with the first major challenge to his company. In April of 1990, the bottom dropped out of the R/C car market. It did not take long to realize that Horizon needed a new business model. No longer could the company prosper as a "middleman"—it needed to have products to sell that were exclusive to Horizon, high quality, and unlike those sold by others.

Rick reached rock bottom as every effort to change Horizon's business model failed. He and his team were out of ideas. Rick saw this as his low point as a leader. Drawing on his biblical knowledge, he saw himself making the same mistake as Moses, when Moses listened to the majority sentiment and decided not to enter the Promised Land. Just as the Israelites were frozen into inaction because of fear, Rick and his team chose to double down on the status quo.

A new opportunity unexpectantly appeared when a wealthy owner of an R/C distributor and direct mail company contacted Rick about buying Horizon Hobby. Rick was unwilling to give up ownership of Horizon, so he turned the tables and offered to buy the wealthy owner's R/C companies instead. In Rick's words, it was a "bet-the-farm" kind of risk. It would either give Horizon the new business model they needed to thrive into the future, or it would lead them into bankruptcy. Through prayer, Rick decided to use holding a hard line on the price to pay for the seller's inventory as a sign to tell him if buying this company was within God's plan. After much intense negotiation, his mark was met. Rick entered this next phase of his business with a sense of excitement and trepidation.

Key Bible Verse

Numbers 13:17-14:10 (read in your own Bible)

Discussion Questions

1. Do you agree with Rick that God is good, but He isn't safe? What does this statement mean to you?

2. On page 70, Rick says, "My life on Earth was tangible and real, but one drastically limited compared to living it with God. Life became more robust and profound when my physical experiences were framed within the context of God's love and His plan for me." What is meant by this quote?

3. The bottom dropped out of the R/C car market in 1990. This part of the market had driven much of Horizon's success. Now Horizon was in a tough spot. Have you experienced this kind of market loss in your company? What was your business response? What was your faith response?

4. How does Rick's fear—driven by personal anxiety and depression—push him towards finding security, the safer route? Can you relate to Rick's dilemma?

5. Take some time to think about Rick's very personal style of prayer. Think about how he listens for God's voice and, once he hears it, seeks to follow it. What can you learn from Rick on this point as a leader of a company or organization?

Rick's Life Lessons

". . . God is good, but He isn't safe. It's 'dangerous' to be around Him because He leads us into risks we would never take ourselves. But oh, what an adventure it is to follow Him and experience the joy of doing more than we ever thought we could!" (p. 69)

"I consider this era to be my leadership at its worst. Organizations don't succeed when decisions are made by consensus. This has been proven time and again in history, and in the stories we read in the Bible about God's dealings with the nation of Israel. When there is a lack of strong leadership the void always gets filled, and it usually gets filled with the loudest voices who are the last ones to provide good leadership." (p. 74)

"It's a good thing I didn't know what lay ahead or I never would have pulled the trigger. I think that's the way God works, though. He knows that if in the beginning I had seen the deep valley to come, I would have taken another route—a safer route—like Moses when he turned back from going into the Promised Land." (p. 78)

Chapter 7: Hitting Rock Bottom

Chapter Synopsis

Making the deal to buy HD seemed like the game changer Horizon needed to start to grow again. Acquiring exclusive products and eliminating a competitor created a new business model for Rick's company and pointed Horizon in a positive direction. Additionally, the answers to prayer that occurred during the purchase process led Rick to believe that it would be much smoother sailing from here on. He could not have been more wrong.

Futaba USA almost immediately dropped Horizon as their distributor out of fear that Horizon would not prioritize Futaba products as they had in the past. This cost Rick's company nearly 20 percent of its revenue stream. This loss, plus other business miscalculations resulting from the deal, put Horizon in worse position than before the purchase of HD.

Believing he had clearly heard God's direction to buy HD, Rick fell into an emotional and spiritual tailspin as his business spiraled downward. He experienced anxiety and depression at unprecedented levels. By 1992, the forty-four-year-old Rick Stephens was spent, and so was his wife. Unbeknownst to Rick, the cumulation of the years of unrelenting emotional toll on Jeanene was causing her to contemplate leaving him. However, God did not leave Rick to dangle in the winds of emotional and spiritual distress beyond what he could handle. At just the right moment, the Spirit of God prompted Rick to resolve to change.

Through the helpful guidance of his counselor, Rick came to realize that he had to learn to live in the moment. It was only in the "here and now" that he could truly walk with God and experience the abundant life the Bible promised. And, again unbeknownst to Rick, Jeanene had decided to give him one more chance.

After reviewing why he had bought HD, and his strong belief that God had confirmed it was the right thing to do, he started to focus on the strengths of the deal. He now had high-quality, under-marketed, exclusive products to sell. Progress was slow to come, but within a few years Horizon started to grow again as the new business model began to move the company into a more prosperous future.

Key Bible Verses

John 10: 10b

I have come that they may have life, and have it to the full.

Philippians 4:6-7

Do not be anxious about anything, but in every situation, by prayer and petition, with thanksgiving, present your requests to God. And the peace of God, which transcends all understanding, will guard your hearts and your minds in Christ Jesus.

Discussion Questions

1. Rick received a "fifteen-word fax" from Futaba, ending their partnership with Horizon Hobby. Have you ever received the equivalent of this "fifteen-word fax"? How did you respond?

2. Rick seemed to miscalculate in two different areas when he purchased HD. Why do you think he did not anticipate these outcomes? What could have blinded him to these possibilities?

3. "I was angry with God and prayed, 'I don't get it! How could You let this happen? I prayed throughout this entire process and felt like You were leading me to buy HD. But look at where we are now! How could You do this to me?'" How do you respond when you are angry at God? Is it okay to respond to God in anger? Read Psalm 6:3, 6 and 10:1, Jeremiah 12:1, and Habakkuk 1:2 for more insight, and discuss what you learn.

4. Rick lays out several practical steps he uses when dealing with depression and anxiety. Do any of these resonate with you? If you have experienced feelings like Rick did/does, how do you deal with it?

   • Smile
   • Reach out to others
   • Just do it
   • Participate, don't spectate
   • Count my blessings

5. "The real story is that God had a plan and every time I trusted Him enough to follow my gut, to follow His Spirit within me, I moved closer to that plan. Whenever I felt like I could figure it out on my own or just didn't have time for God, I wandered around in the wilderness for a while. But it was all part of the long journey with

Him." (p. 89) How do you respond to Rick's concluding thoughts. What do they make you think about?

Rick's Life Lessons

"Have you ever noticed that God loves to show up when a situation seems impossible? It seems to me that's where He often does His best work—in impossible situations." (p. 81)

"At that moment a thought came to mind, maybe from the Holy Spirit, 'Rick, you've lived forty-four years controlled by your circumstances, high as a kite one day and hitting rock bottom the next. You'll probably live to be about eighty-eight years old, so half of your life has been spent thinking about how bad things are or how bad things could be. It's time to stop it!" I did not want to live the next forty-four years of my life depressed. I had to do something different." (p. 83)

"Rick, you're always ruminating about the past or worrying about the future. You never live in the present." (p. 84)

Chapter 8: Leading a Culture, Not Just a Company

Chapter Synopsis

To stay competitive in the industry, Horizon continued to evolve with the marketplace. Rick decided to purchase a mail-order company so Horizon could sell directly to the consumer. Cashing in on the personal trust he had built over the years, his sales team and hobby store owners gave Horizon the space it needed to grow the company.

Looking back, Rick realized that a key component to Horizon's success was its openness to changing its business model every five to eight years. Starting with its founding in 1985, Horizon had made significant changes in 1992, 1998, and 2004. This sort of business innovation emerged from its bi-annual strategic planning retreats. These retreats also allowed Rick to build the culture he envisioned at Horizon, including the concept of servant leadership. Horizon was God's company and as its leader, Rick needed to practice the kind of servant leadership that the Bible described.

Key Bible Verse

Jesus is the ultimate example of servant leadership. Read and think about the following passage:

Philippians 2: 5-8:

In your relationships with one another, have the same mindset as Christ Jesus: Who, being in very nature God, did not consider equality with God something to be used to his own advantage; rather, he made himself nothing by taking the very nature of a servant, being made in human likeness. And being found in appearance as a man, he humbled himself by becoming obedient to death—even death on a cross!

(Rick also strongly recommends that business leaders read the Old Testament book of Nehemiah and study Nehemiah's example of servant leadership.)

Discussion Questions

1. When Rick needed to reset Horizon's business model to remain competitive, employees and customers trusted him. Personal integrity plays a significant role when you ask people to do something extraordinary. What does personal integrity look like to you? Can you provide an example of a time when personal integrity helped your business or organization?

2. What message did Rick send to his sales team when he joined them to make the difficult telephone calls to dealers?

3. "Honest, direct, and consistent communication resolves a lot of issues in advance and inspires trust. This is true in business and it's true in personal situations." Discuss this statement from Rick.

4. Horizon refreshed its business model every five to eight years. As you reflect on your company, how often have you made changes to your business model that led to new growth?

5. What do you think of the leadership model known as "servant leadership"? Take a moment to do a personal inventory of your servant leadership capacity. On a scale of 1 to 10, with 10 being the highest, how would you rate yourself as a servant leader?

   _____ Shares power
   _____ Provides employees all they need to be successful

_____ Is not self-serving

_____ Listens to others

_____ Attaches value to their ideas

_____ Does not blame others

_____ Leads thoughtfully and decisively

_____ Provides clear direction

_____ Holds people accountable

_____ Inspires people to follow him or her

_____ Is always prepared, trustworthy, caring, and honest

Rick's Life Lessons

"As I look back over the history of Horizon, I realize that every five to eight years, we needed a significant change in our business model in order to optimize the business." (p. 95)

"Often the leader is the expert and heavily invested in the products sold. But leading people and running a business with excellence is what I was heavily invested in—not the products themselves. My priority was genuinely loving people, providing resources for them to use their skills successfully, dreaming bigger than humanly possible, and achieving excellence in everything we did." (pp. 97)

"A servant leader shares power, provides employees all they need to be successful, and helps people be the best they can be. A servant leader is not self-serving, but listens to others and attaches value to their ideas. A servant leader doesn't blame others, bring others down to make himself look better, or try to 'beat' others. A servant leader wants to win as a team." (p. 98)

". . . we found that servant leadership is a hard thing to teach. The force behind the authority of a servant leader is leading by example. If one doesn't start with the motivation to serve others first, it's not likely they will become a servant leader." (p. 99)

Chapter 9: Ultimate Faith

Chapter Synopsis

Rick experienced "Ultimate Faith" through the fatal illness of his son-in-law, Matt, the husband of his eldest daughter, Jill. The first marriage of his three daughters taught Rick the awkwardness that accompanies the transference of a daughter's first love for her father to that of her husband. Yet, there were moments when Jill's love for her father was made clear. Fond memories were made throughout her youth, and this was affirmed when Jill chose to be married at the Chapel in Snowmass, Colorado—a second home for the family. The realization that Jill had chosen such a good man in Matt—one who understood what it means to love Jesus—made it easier for Rick to let go.

Tragedy struck a year later when Matt was diagnosed with cancer. The Stephens family moved into full action, but there was nothing anyone could do to fully solve the crisis. Matt's faith shone brightly during this trial by fire, setting an example for all, especially Rick. In this way, Matt indirectly took on the unexpected role of spiritual mentor to Rick. During the trying final months, Matt became more incapacitated, and Rick was tasked with reading the Bible to him. These times together were poignant for Rick's personal faith. As the end approached, Rick learned what it takes to face the ultimate uncertainty of death. It was Matt's ultimate and unwavering faith in Christ that saw the family through this painful time.

Key Bible Verse

Matthew 14:27

But Jesus immediately said to them: "Take courage! It is I. Don't be afraid."

Discussion Questions

1. Describe the strength and health of the Stephens family as they rallied around their daughter and son-in-law during this tragic period. What were some of the building blocks in the family's history that made this possible?

2. Rick described how God even used Matt's tribulation to do His work. What impressed you most about the positives that came out of this negative experience? What does the Bible say about suffering and its redeeming qualities?

3. First Corinthians 13:13 speaks to the reality that in Christ we have faith, hope, and love. How do you see these bedrock promises of God demonstrated in Matt's story?

4. Rick revealed that the experience of Matt's tragic battle with cancer deeply influenced how he came to view life and death. What do we learn in this chapter about how this experience changed Rick?

5. Matt's death was not the end of Jill's life. In what ways did God continue to bless her?

Rick's Life Lessons

"We naturally become anxious and afraid when faced with uncertainty, and death is the ultimate uncertainty. Yet, one of the most repeated phrases in the Bible is, 'Do not be afraid.' I believe God is telling me, *I know you can't see into the future but I can, and it will be okay. I created you and know what I'm doing. You can depend on the fact that I've got the next stage of your life taken care of.*" (p. 108)

"The only way I know to counteract the ultimate uncertainty is through ultimate faith . . . When we accept there is a bigger picture than what man sees and God is in control of it all, we have the kind of faith Matt demonstrated and I strive for—ultimate faith." (p. 109)

"Whether it's family or career, bad things happen and good things happen. We must accept both in stride. The trick is to find ways to enjoy life—and each other—when disaster strikes, and not get too carried away when things break in our favor. Life is never as bad as it seems when in the valley, nor as good as it seems at other times." (p. 109)

Chapter 10: Navigating Success

Chapter Synopsis

Rick overrode plenty of internal skepticism at Horizon to hire Silicon Valley inventor Paul Beard as Vice President of Engineering in 2004. Beard's hiring marked another milestone in the growth of Horizon as a company. Soon, Horizon became an innovator of new technology for RC merchandise. With the development of Spektrum, the company became a pacesetter in the worldwide RC hobby business. The new technological advantages of Spektrum pushed Horizon over the top as a leading innovative company in the industry.

Topping $200 million in annual revenue, the company (and Rick personally) started to experience the pros and cons of success. For the company, they now had the "good problem" of maintaining their position as an innovative leader. For Rick and Jeanene, new complications emerged when they felt some acquaintances looked at them differently because of their new social and economic status. They also wrestled with the guilt of "Why me?" as they learned how to live with more money than they ever expected. As they sought God for guidance, Rick and Jeanene began to learn how to invest wisely as they gave their money away to help others, fulfilling the Great Commandment.

Key Bible Verse/Quote

Luke 12:48b

From everyone who has been given much, much will be demanded; and from the one who has been entrusted with much, much more will be asked.

"And if we distribute to the needy, we shall obtain for ourselves great abundance. And for this it is that God has permitted you to possess much, not that you should spend it in fornication, in drunkenness, in gluttony, in rich clothing, or any other mode of luxury, but that you should distribute it to the needy."

— John Chrysostom, *On Wealth and Poverty*

Discussion Questions

1. Twice, Rick had to overcome the obstacle of trying to lead people outside their "comfort zone"—first, with his own product development department and then, with his friends at JR Radios. What enabled him to do this? How do you lead people outside their "comfort zone" (including yourself!)?

2. One does not often think of God as innovative or disruptive, but what stories from the Bible might display these qualities in Him? In what way(s) is God never innovative or disruptive?

3. As Rick achieved greater success at Horizon, he noticed that some people started to treat him differently. Have you experienced this in your own life when you've experienced success? How have you handled it? What does the Bible teach about handling success?

4. "Giving leads to contentment." Rick speaks to the problems of growing wealth in this chapter. What are some takeaways from his experience that you can apply to your own life, whether gaining wealth yourself or watching others do so?

5. What do you think the connection is between generosity and self-centeredness? Can the former alleviate the latter? Share your experiences.

Rick's Life Lessons

"Giving generously made us feel like maybe the reason God had blessed us financially was so we could bless others. We never again had any trouble giving 10 percent of our personal income away and our guilt of having more than others disappeared with the giving. We felt enormously blessed that we got to keep 90 percent of what He had provided!" (p. 117)

"I've found that giving is the antidote to self-centeredness and a lot of other things in life I don't want to be . . . The very act of giving takes my eyes off myself and puts them on others." (p. 117)

"Comparatively, generosity is the opposite of being devoted to oneself. I would argue the extent of one's generosity actually defines the extent of one's ability to live abundantly." (p. 119)

"Generous people are able to experience abundant life. Without generosity, we are unable to let go of selfishness." (p. 119)

"However, we are also comfortable using some for ourselves and believe that serves a purpose too. We don't feel guilt for having nice things, as long as they are shared with others and don't interfere with giving to those in need." (p. 119)

Chapter 11: Succession Planning

Chapter Synopsis

Around the year 2000, Rick began to think about succession planning. This was a lengthy process he found to be quite difficult. Though he put a lot of energy and talent into the process, every step was fraught with uncertainty, lack of clear direction, and countless failures. His quest to find a successor and build a structure that would carry on his vision for Horizon after his departure eventually led to a 100 percent ESOP (Employee Stock Ownership Plan). This created the structure needed to pass the company on and rewarded those who had helped make Horizon a success. However, he still had not found a leader whom he believed understood and embraced the purpose of Horizon.

In the end, Rick's ambivalence about stepping down from his position as CEO undoubtedly clouded his perspective. Rick never felt like he had clear guidance from God but eventually settled on Joe as CEO and tried to move on to the next phase of his life. (Of special note is the role his brother Larry played in the Horizon story and the great love of one brother for another.)

Key Bible Verses

Judges 6:17

Gideon replied, "If now I have found favor in your eyes, give me a sign that it is really you talking to me."

Isaiah 38:22

Hezekiah had asked, "What will be the sign that I will go up to the temple of the Lord?"

Discussion Questions

1. Rick wrote, "In hindsight I believe that Horizon might have been better off with Janet in that role after me, even without the business training." (p. 122) Think also about James 3:17: "But the wisdom that comes from heaven is first of all pure; then peace-loving, considerate, submissive, full of mercy and good fruit, impartial and sincere." What value do you place on technical skills (competency) versus character or commitment when hiring and promoting people in your company? How did Larry's role exemplify this principle in Rick's life?

2. Rick believes you can tell a lot about a leader by the people they hire. Take a moment to think about those whom you have hired to work for you. What does it say about your leadership?

3. Rick always sought confirmation signs from God when he was making a big decision. What do you think of this approach to seeking God? What direction does the Bible provide for this approach?

4. What do you think of the ESOP as a tool for succession planning? What are some alternative models you like better?

5. Throughout the whole process of succession planning, the company continued to grow, bringing in $335 million by the fall of 2012. Did this continued growth make it easier or more difficult for Rick to let go? How do you think it would affect you?

Rick's Life Lessons

"Today I would probably look at this differently. History has shown me that having the right vision, values, and leadership ability is more important than understanding business, especially in a company like Horizon that puts values before anything else. Business skills can be taught; character cannot." (p. 122)

"I learned later that he had prayed about it long and hard. Eventually, he felt like he heard a message that Horizon was my call from God, and his call from God was to help and support me. In other words, he believed God was telling him to take a back seat to his younger brother. Larry quietly gave up the role of President/CEO but continued to do all he could to make me and Horizon successful. How many people would do that?" (p. 123)

"As any entrepreneur reading this knows, when you start an organization and run it for almost thirty years, you have a feel for what's going on deep inside the belly of a company that no one else understands. You can feel it when things aren't right . . . and I could feel that things were definitely not right." (p. 131)

Chapter 12: Letting Go

Chapter Synopsis

When Rick learned from Horizon's CEO that it would not meet its loan covenant requirements at the end of the quarter, he jumped back into the day-to-day operations of the company. The problem: he was the Chairman of the Board, and not the CEO of Horizon. The overstepping of his authority brought Rick's involvement at Horizon to a head. He decided he must become CEO again or sell the company, in order to protect his family's investment. His gut told him it was time to disentangle himself once and for all, but he had a strong desire to jump in and rescue his "baby." He looked for a sign from God and got it when the board decided he should let Joe lead. One year later, the sale of Horizon Hobby was completed.

Even though the closure of this chapter of his life was bittersweet, Rick was proud of Horizon's accomplishments. Not only did it make hundreds of Horizonites more secure financially, but Rick's early prayer that Horizon be God's company was validated by all those who deepened their faith in Jesus while working at the company. He could leave in peace knowing Horizon had fulfilled its vision "to see the world impacted by God through the influence of Horizon and its people." After twenty-eight years as the head of a dynamic, worldwide company, Rick rested in his confidence that God had more for him to do—that this was not the end of the journey. Claiming the promise of Psalm 92:12-15, Rick looked to his future with excitement: "They will still bear fruit in old age, they will stay fresh and green."

Key Bible Verse

Psalm 92:12-15

The righteous will flourish like a palm tree, they will grow like a cedar of Lebanon; planted in the house of the Lord, they will flourish in the courts of our God. They will still bear fruit in old age, they will stay fresh and green, proclaiming, "The Lord is upright; he is my Rock, and there is no wickedness in him."

Discussion Questions

1. When Rick encountered a problem, whether business-related or personal, he consistently sought God for direction and wisdom. As he grappled with succession, he took a personal two-week spiritual retreat to seek God about his future. Are there any elements about the retreat that stood out to you as especially helpful? Have you ever taken a spiritual retreat?

2. "I don't want you to DO anything, Rick! I just want you to devote yourself to Me." Why did Rick need to hear this message from God? What do you think it meant to him?

3. What must it have been like for the CEO to have Rick as the Chairman of the Board? What could have been done to create a better working relationship between these two? Any thoughts on how the board handled the situation between Rick and the CEO, and Rick and Horizon?

4. The selling of Horizon Hobby was bittersweet for Rick and Jeanene. What can we learn from this process?

5. Rick concluded the sale of Horizon with a summary statement about the business and spiritual benefits the company created.

Take a few minutes and write a summary statement you hope to write for your company or business when the time comes for you to leave.

Rick's Life Lessons

"It's probably obvious by now, but I love to work. The day I find myself without an important project or meaningful purpose for any length of time is the day I will feel like my life on Earth is nearing completion. I cherish time spent with family and enjoy travel, fine food, golf, and having fun with friends. But making something special happen that improves the lives of others is what drives me. If I was being called to let Horizon go, I needed to fill the void." (p. 133)

"Our company had also been a wonderful ministry. Some people accepted Christ for the first time, some grew much closer to God, some had opportunities to learn about God and hear from Him who might not have otherwise. Spiritual outcomes are not so easy to measure, but everyone who came in our door saw something different about Horizon and I like to think they saw the love of God in our people. Our vision had been fulfilled: 'To see the world impacted by God through the influence of Horizon and its people.'" (p. 142)

"There is no greater privilege than to be used by God to accomplish His purposes. What He requires of us is to stay connected to Him, living in dependence on His limitless resources. Then, He is able to work through us to transform and make better the lives of those around us. We are grateful that God showed His constant presence as we journeyed to our Promised Land." (p. 142)

Chapter 13: Family Matters

Chapter Synopsis

Rick struggled with his work/life balance, concluding that there is not "any easy, black-and-white answer for leaders who are navigating this tension." (p. 153) Still, there was much Rick had to learn along the way. First, he noted how important it is to have a loving spouse who is willing to call you out when you fall short. Second, he discussed how your spouse can empower you when he/she knows how to play to your strengths. Jeanene did not simply criticize Rick for his lack of attention to her life and their daughters—she suggested a strategy for him to follow that would make him a better husband and father.

Jeanene knew that Rick was a detail-oriented leader who kept a manila folder on every important facet at work. So, she strongly suggested this same approach to help Rick fulfill his duties as the *pater familias*. This novel approach worked well for Rick, moving him closer to realizing what he honestly believed: family comes first. It not only helped him stay more involved in the lives of his daughters but helped him develop necessary structures for a better work/life balance.

It took decades to arrive at this point—the point in his life when his daughters were grown, married, and raising families—but Rick can say with full candor that at "this time of my life, I understand better than ever the importance of family." (p. 155) Through it all, he said, "the best times of life for me are still whenever I'm with Jeanene." (p. 156)

Key Bible Verses

Psalm 5:3

In the morning, LORD, you hear my voice; in the morning I lay my requests before you and wait expectantly.

1 John 5:14

This is the confidence we have in approaching God: that if we ask anything according to his will, he hears us.

Discussion Questions

1. Rick is an example of someone who has tried to saturate his life with prayer. What do you think it takes to develop this approach to Christian living?

2. Most of this chapter deals with Rick's struggles to find a work/life balance. How are you doing with your own work/life balance? What are your biggest struggles? Write down three takeaways from Rick's journey towards a better work/life balance.

3. Take a moment to do a personal work/life balance inventory. On a scale of 1 to 10, with 10 being the best, how would you rate yourself?

    _____ You know your spouse's love language.
    _____ You are teaching your children a healthy perspective about money and how to manage it.
    _____ You spend quality time with your children.
    _____ You spend quantity time with your children.
    _____ You know your children's schedules for the next week.

_____ You cultivate your relationship with your wife by taking periodic "date nights."

_____ You take time away from work.

4. "Throughout my career, I felt God nudging me as He walked beside me. He was my inner companion with a full understanding of my life, my family's needs, and my own personal struggles." (p. 152) Take time to think about this statement. What sort of desires does it evoke inside of you?

5. Explore how Rick the owner/CEO and Rick the grandfather are similar. How are they different?

Rick's Life Lessons

"Sometimes I have thought that prayer is awkward or unnecessary. It's so easy to skip, and it would have been my usual behavior to let that moment early in the morning at OU pass right on by. _Every little thing_ doesn't need to be prayed about, right? But experiences like these tell me God is listening and wants to be a part of every thought I have, big or small." (p. 146)

"Yes, I was driven—driven by my desire to do it all and do it all with excellence. I understood the critical importance of my role in the family, but it was a constant challenge to perform well in all my capacities: as husband, father, leader at Horizon, and community volunteer." (p. 147)

"If you'd asked me at the time, I would have verbally acknowledged I believed that 'family comes first.' But, truthfully . . . my actions didn't show it." (p. 148)

"That's why this strategic and intentional shift in priorities was so important to me. I wish it had been more natural for me to give my family the attention they deserved, regardless of the pull of other responsibilities, but I had to work at it. Every step I took—whether it was to call a family meeting to order, help orchestrate a family trip, or be there to talk with Jeanene and the girls about what was important to them—was purposeful, because I knew God was calling me to improve in this area of my life and my family deserved better than I was giving them." (p. 152)

Chapter 14: Dream Big

Chapter Synopsis

Rick and Jeanene began their post-Horizon life by building on prior volunteer work. God had been planting seeds and making connections all along that began to bear unforeseen fruit after Rick sold Horizon. In 2008, Rick and Jeanene were approached to help lead a campaign to build a recreational facility in Champaign for those with disabilities. Seeing a chance to fulfill their constant prayer that their dreams be God-sized, an opportunity developed to work with the YMCA to build a completely reconceptualized Y—one that would be especially designed for families affected by disability. So, instead of different people going different ways for recreation, this Y would bring all kinds of people together—especially those with disabilities and those without. However, the financial commitment was immense. The new Y would cost $18 million. It was indeed a God-sized dream.

An amazing story followed about a community that came together to catch the vision and raise the money for the project. Personally, for Rick and Jeanene, this project was the culmination of a story that God had been weaving into the fabric of their lives for many years. God had planted seeds within them through Aspen Challenge and a very special relationship with a young lady named Marnie. God was working out His plans even when they did not know it.

Soon after the completion of the Y, God showed them He had even more projects in mind. When the Chancellor of the University of Illinois (UIUC) came knocking on their door, they suddenly found themselves swept into another God-sized story. Called upon to help build community support for an innovative new medical school, Rick and Jeanene knew that the Savior who loves to heal was again at work in their lives.

Key Bible Verse

Matthew 25:40

The King will reply, "Truly I tell you, whatever you did for one of the least of these brothers and sisters of mine, you did for me."

Discussion Questions

1. Connect the dots in Rick and Jeanene's life that led to their role in the building of the newly conceptualized YMCA in Champaign. What do you observe about how God works in our lives? What kind of seeds do you see God planting in your life?

2. Led by Rick and Jeanene, the team that oversaw the campaign to build the new YMCA was motivated by Christian faith. Putting Christ at the center of the project created a few issues with those in the larger community who wanted to make the focus more broad, not based on the love of Jesus for others. Have you faced similar obstacles in your life or in community projects of which you were a part? On this point, what can you learn from the example of the building of the new YMCA?

3. "This was going to be fun—I knew God would do it again. We just didn't believe anything could be too big for God." (p. 162) How is this sort of faith cultivated? What experiences have caused your own faith to grow?

4. Rick's brother, Larry, stepped up to help Rick again on the YMCA project. Take a few minutes to reflect on the critical role Larry played in Rick's life. How does this motivate you to be a better brother or sibling?

5. Rick had the capacity to dedicate himself to many worthy projects. Based on his story, what do you think are the motivating factors behind the projects he chose to invest in? What can you learn from his example?

Rick's Life Lessons

"We [Rick and Jeanene] wanted His dreams to become our dreams, and we wanted those dreams to be God-sized. God more than honored our desire." (p. 157)

"No, none of it 'just happened.' It all became part of a plan that was laid out long before any of us knew anything about it. God had a plan to help the 'least of these' in our community and gave us the opportunity to join in His work. We took a giant step of faith forward, even though we couldn't see what was ahead. The result was an amazing accomplishment that some said couldn't be done—but God . . . " (p. 165)

"Jeanene and I aren't any more comfortable taking risks than the next person . . . Without knowing God and having a personal relationship with Him, without a spiritual life running in tandem with our physical life, we most certainly would have chosen safer routes. But oh, what excitement and joy we would have missed if our dreams had been limited to what we could see and understand." (p. 168)

Chapter 15: Relationships

Chapter Synopsis

What was the secret of Rick's success? God first, then family, friends, and colleagues. A personal relationship with God and a storehouse of friendships added up to abundant life.

It is not the highs and lows of life that define who you are or determine the sort of life you experience—it is the relationships you carry. Relationships determine how you understand the life around you. Whether it's the loss of a job, the low points of building and sustaining a company, or the death of someone close to you, God can redeem even the worst moments in your life when they are viewed through His lens.

Similarly, great friendships (like the ones Rick had with Jeanene, his brother Larry, and Tim Johnson) can support us through life's trials and add the spice that gives life its zest. But, underneath it all is a personal relationship with God—a relationship that takes time to cultivate but pays off in extraordinary ways. Jesus is the catalyst that makes this abundant life possible!

Key Bible Verse

Matthew 6:33
But seek first his kingdom and his righteousness, and all these things will be given to you as well.

Discussion Questions

1. Rick and Tim Johnson shared a passion for the work of God as it relates to Christian ministry and the culture of business. If that is what drew them together, what was it about their relationship that took it to the next level?

2. Rick stressed the positive impact of small groups on his business and spiritual life. He especially emphasized the importance of confidentiality and commitment. Do you agree with his analysis about small groups and their impact? What role have small groups played in your business and spiritual life?

3. Rick wrote more about his involvement with nonprofits, parachurch ministries, and community projects than he did about his participation in the local church. Would you consider these entities more entrepreneurial and innovative than the typical local church? If this is true, how do you think the local church might utilize the skills and gifts of an entrepreneur?

4. Rick wrote, "I used to believe that showing any kind of vulnerability to others would shatter their confidence in me and my ability to lead them. But I came to understand that the strongest leaders are those with enough self-confidence to acknowledge their strengths and weaknesses and build a team around them with people able to perform far better than themselves in areas of weakness" (p. 176). On a scale of 1 to 10, with 10 being the best, how are you doing in this area of leadership? Explain.

5. Rick lays out several practical steps on how to grow in your personal relationship with God. What are they, and how fitting are they for you? What other practices work for you?

Rick's Life Lessons

". . . life is all about relationships. Throughout my life, it's been the people around me who have shaped me and given me joy. I believe we are wired to connect to God and other people from the time we're babies, and living abundantly depends on healthy, vibrant, and meaningful relationships." (p. 169)

"There are a few people in life you can trust with *anything*. If you have a handful of real friends whom you know will stand with you no matter what, you are a fortunate person. Tim is one of those people for me. We've encouraged each other, cried together, worked on projects together, prayed together, and challenged each other when we're wrong. He has mentored me and I him for almost three decades, and we wouldn't be the men we are today without our investment in each other." (p. 171)

"Our desire to engage in the community and its leaders stems from our belief that biblical truths work just as well in secular organizations as they do in Christian organizations, and a community thrives when these truths are applied in both." (p. 171)

". . . I've come to believe that *anything good that happens, happens through a small group.*" (p. 172)

"That's what my life is all about. Doing my best to stay on course to live well physically and spiritually at the same time. Surrounding myself with relationships that push me forward, edify, and build me up. Because that is how we experience abundant life. The best life. With others, and with God." (p. 180)

Chapter 16: The Secret of My Success

Chapter Synopsis

In this concluding chapter, Rick distilled for us the most important life lessons he learned as a business entrepreneur and disciple of Jesus Christ. "Biblical principles just work—it's as simple as that" (p. 181). As the saying goes, what is simple is not always easy. Rick emphasized this principle in both the building of Horizon Hobby and the following of Jesus.

For Rick, giving his all meant no silos, no compartmentalizing, no separating career from faith, and no mediocre efforts. He wanted, above all, to live the abundant life that Christ promised in John 10:10. This did not necessarily mean riches, fame, or power. For Rick, getting the most out of life boiled down to one simple statement. He said, "My definition of Abundant Life is where I'm in alignment with my Creator—when I feel close to Him, and when I see His Hand all over what is happening in my physical life."

Rick sees a person's physical life without God to be like experiencing a two-dimensional movie. With God, however, every part of life can take on a sharpness—a depth, a broader meaning—akin to experiencing that same movie, only now in a 3D theatre. Rick pointed us to the Scriptures to acquire a perfect understanding of life lived simultaneously in the physical and spiritual realms. Through Christ, the two worlds come together perfectly.

Rick wrote, "The truth is, making Christ the bedrock of my career has led to greater success than I would have ever imagined—in business, with my family, and at play." (p. 187) He concluded by inviting the reader to embark on the same adventure. Of course, others' journeys won't look the same as his, but they will produce the same abundant life.

Key Bible Verse

Matthew 6:9-13

This, then, is how you should pray: "Our Father in heaven, hallowed be your name, your kingdom come, your will be done, on earth as it is in heaven. Give us today our daily bread. And forgive us our debts, as we also have forgiven our debtors. And lead us not into temptation, but deliver us from the evil one."

Discussion Questions

1. Rick worked hard to create company values that were biblical. The three values at Horizon were: 1) The Golden Rule, 2) The Customer Is Boss, and 3) The Inverted Pyramid Organizational Chart. What similarities and differences do you see between your company values and Horizon Hobby's?

2. Rick gave his definition of abundant life in this chapter. What is your definition of abundant life? Has the reading of this book shifted your understanding in any way?

3. We learned in this chapter that Rick was intimidated when he first started reading the Bible. How comfortable are you with reading the Bible? What might help you to understand the Bible better?

4. On page 187, Rick laid out Henry Blackaby's "Seven Realities" on God's involvement in a person's physical life. Reflect on some major

events in your life in terms of these "Seven Realities." Describe how these seven points took form in one of your major events.

5. Rick has had the unique opportunity to work and live alongside many high-capacity leaders. He passionately believes that many of them have missed out on their best life because they "settle" for financial success, power, influence, fame, or something else from this physical life. Evaluate your motivations for the things you do and try to determine how close or far you are from the abundant life.

Rick's Life Lessons

"I didn't want to 'play' at living my spiritual life by giving it lip service, attending church, and doing enough good deeds to make my scorecard with God look good. I wanted to give it my all." (p. 182)

"My physical life is strong and I'm going to squeeze every drop out of it I can. But it remains finite, and everything I accumulate and enjoy in this physical life will come to an end. My spiritual life, on the other hand, is infinite. It adds greater depth to every experience of physical life. Why would I ever be satisfied living my life within physical limits when it offers only a fraction of the possibilities?" (p. 187)

"The truth is that making Christ the bedrock of my career has led to greater success than I would have ever imagined—in business, with my family, and at play. I see so many high-capacity leaders settle for less than what life has to offer because they think they have it all figured out. They lock their eyes on financial success, power, influence, fame, family, or something else from this physical life and they may do it really well. All the while, they are missing the entire spiritual dimension of life." (p. 187)

"I'm talking about the joy and fulfillment that come from an integrated physical and spiritual life, lived in relationship with God and alignment with His Word. God is right there, in plain sight, waiting to offer you the fullest, most abundant life you can imagine." (p. 189)

ABOUT THE AUTHOR

Rick Stephens is a successful entrepreneur and business leader who is passionate and purposeful about making faith in God the central part of his business and career. His commitment to excellence in both corporate and non-profit environments—combined with his desire to teach leaders to become even better leaders—are the driving forces in his life.

He is the founder of Horizon Hobby Inc., a hobby distribution business that, over the course of 28 years, became a world leader in the design and development of hobby products, including radio control airplanes, helicopters, and cars, model railroad equipment, and general hobby items. Horizon grew to exceed $335 million in revenues with over 700 people and facilities in Illinois, California, London, Hamburg, and Shanghai. In 2006, Horizon became 100 percent employee-owned and in 2014, sold to private equity on behalf of the employees.

Rick has served on numerous boards including the Radio Control Hobby Trade Association, Fellowship of Christian Athletes, Young President's Organization, Carle Hospital Foundation, University of Illinois Foundation, University of Illinois Research Park, Stephens Family YMCA, Pinnacle Forum, and Lead Like Jesus.

Since he ended his career with Horizon, Rick and his wife Jeanene have established Investres, LLC, with the purpose of investing their time and resources in three areas: people, projects, and possibilities. This has led to the Stephens Family YMCA, a Guest House for an orphanage in Haiti, co-chairing Vision 2020 (a $35 million campaign to transform healthcare through innovative medicine and compassionate care), and active personal investments.

Rick and Jeanene have been married 49 years and treasure time with their three daughters, three sons-in-law, and eight grandchildren. They enjoy leading forum groups for personal and spiritual growth and mentoring leaders, as well as travel, golf, hiking, and snowboarding.

www.ricklstephens.com

A free ebook edition is available with the purchase of this book.

To claim your free ebook edition:

1. Visit MorganJamesBOGO.com
2. Sign your name CLEARLY in the space
3. Complete the form and submit a photo of the entire copyright page
4. You or your friend can download the ebook to your preferred device

Morgan James
BOGO™

A **FREE** ebook edition is available for you or a friend with the purchase of this print book.

CLEARLY SIGN YOUR NAME ABOVE

Instructions to claim your free ebook edition:
1. Visit MorganJamesBOGO.com
2. Sign your name CLEARLY in the space above
3. Complete the form and submit a photo of this entire page
4. You or your friend can download the ebook to your preferred device

Print & Digital Together Forever.

Snap a photo

Free ebook

Read anywhere

Printed in the USA
CPSIA information can be obtained
at www.ICGtesting.com
JSHW022218140824
68134JS00018B/1126